Breaking The Spell

An Exploration of Human Perception

Breaking The Spell

An Exploration of Human Perception

Kingsley L. Dennis

O
BOOKS

Winchester, UK
Washington, USA

First published by O-Books, 2013
O-Books is an imprint of John Hunt Publishing Ltd., Laurel House, Station Approach,
Alresford, Hants, SO24 9JH, UK
office1@jhpbooks.net
www.johnhuntpublishing.com

For distributor details and how to order please visit the 'Ordering' section on our website.

Text copyright: Kingsley L. Dennis 2012

ISBN: 978 1 78099 219 8

A CIP catalogue record for this book is available from the British Library.

Design: Stuart Davies

Printed and bound by CPI Group (UK) Ltd, Croydon, CR0 4YY

We operate a distinctive and ethical publishing philosophy in all
areas of our business, from our global network of authors to
production and worldwide distribution.

CONTENTS

Dedication

Agha (1922 - 2005) - for providing the necessary tools for
breaking the spell

Rahime - for being the perfect spell

Our Intuitive Selves

Human beings have always lived within a world steeped in mysteries and secrets. For most, the gap between our perception and Reality remains unbridgeable. Yet ways, means, and teachings have always existed that have provided access to glimpses of Reality. One of the core secrets contained within this perennial body of knowledge has been that we, as human beings, have *the ability to manipulate our sense of reality*. Further, that this capacity stems from within ourselves and can be developed. In fact, we've always had this potential; we just never knew how to understand it and thus approach it. And if we ever learned how to use it, and were not ready for it, we could cause a great deal of disruption – and distress - for ourselves and our societies. This has always been the 'secret that protects itself'. Yet, at all times, it has never been wholly absent or invisible.

It may be the case that there have always been hints provided. Only that the language wasn't always clear. It couldn't be. There was too much at stake to reveal some of the most potent secrets into the profane sphere. The 'Kingdom of Heaven' was always within. And this has been so from the very beginning. Yet some things got lost along the way... and the world outside of us became so much more enticing than the world within. Human attention became fixed on the outward, exteriorizing the gaze, until there was little else to look at. And so the physical world became the focus for the senses. From archangel to atoms, from magic to materiality, the human spirit slowly seeped away from its imaginative center.

Our far human ancestors saw the world around them very differently. For them, life existed together as a vibrant matrix of connected, living energies. Each stone, flower, buzzing insect, played a role. Each aspect of the cosmos was intrinsically entangled and woven together. All matter, organic or inorganic, was in correspondence. The line between 'living' and 'non-living' was a blurred one in long ages past. There was a sense of communion virtually non-existent today. Nowadays the average person is unaware of the affinities that bind the interior and exterior realms. In one way the physical world was perceived as softer and less defined in our ancient past. Life was permeated by a mosaic of energetic affinities and correspondences. Biology was not restricted to within the membrane of bodies but was bound also to the heavenly movements. Human patterns mirrored their cosmic counterparts. Their rhythms were joined in fusion, influencing human function. Today we know of such correspondences as biorhythms; such as the 24-hour circadian rhythms. Sun, moon, planets, and stars have all been known in ancient times to have their various influences upon the living processes of Earth. Astrology and astrobiology are avenues that seek to understand these connections.

It is said that humans breathe on average 25,920 times per day, the same number of years within a Great Year, or for a full precession of the equinox (the number of years it takes for the sun to complete a full cycle of the Zodiac). Similarly, the average human lifespan of 72 years contains the same number of days. Our far ancient ancestors instinctively knew of such biological interconnectedness. They also recognized the interrelatedness of consciousness, mind, and material reality. In modern terminology, we can say they understood how the field of consciousness acts as an extended mind; how thoughts connect species and groups. Further, that thoughts are not so much created within an individual mind but are impressions received from the interpenetrating collective mind. No thought or action lies separate or without consequence. All of life is inextricably woven together.

Yet perhaps most important of all, the ancients knew that

universal order was a *mind-before-matter* manifestation. In other words, *Mind* was the fundamental basis underlying *Matter*. Connection with a conscious, living universe through internalized affinities and correspondences was thus vital for a harmonious relationship with the external physical world. Matter could be approached through the sphere of the Mind. Creativity was inherent within the power of the imagination, human will, and intention.

The modern industrialized world of the human being today is largely void of this internalized relationship. It rarely comes to our 'mind' that if we limit our vision, we create our own limitations for the endless possibilities around us. In other words, the human 'worlds' we live within can only evolve as far as we have the vision to conceive and connect with it. Without such creative, intuitive and perceptive vision our cultures will eventually fall away and cease to evolve in line with the Earth's evolving change.

Whether we fully appreciate it or not, we choose the manifestation of our world picture. As in the famous 'optical illusion' image that can be seen equally as a pretty young woman or an old hook-nosed hag, our worldview can be pretty or haggard. Thus, how *we view* determines how *we do*...

To be conscious of this process helps us to make our own decisions on how we wish to engage with daily life. We are constantly being asked to choose the level and quality of our involvement - how we use our inner vision to both correspond and respond to our physical circumstances, as well as our cosmic environment.

Our consciousness is already different from that of our parents' consciousness; and probably far beyond that of our grandparents. Already the rate of change in our perceptual paradigms has evolved rapidly. Human forms of consciousness have always evolved (e.g. from the mythical to the mental-rational); yet today they are evolving at an increasingly accelerated pace. Can we envision how our consciousness will change in the near future? This is likely to be greatly influenced by the quality and depth of our intuitive perceptions, and the increasing manifestation of our interior capacities.

Living an interiorized life does not mean retreating inward as would an ascetic or hermit. Rather it is about recognizing, engaging with, and connecting with the living cosmos of which we are a part. This means we interiorize what we feel to be the exterior, physical cosmos. We live with it as part of our every moment as if there is no separation between us and 'it'. The physical distance in between the cosmos and the individual melts and merges into a living unity. By this act of intuitive engagement we request our right to once again become a living, creative part of our larger environment. Perhaps it is now time we broke open our cocoons of the material self by our recognition of the greater living, conscious unity. And by recognizing too the perceptual prisons we are held within.

These 'prisons' that hold us are the *cognitive systems* that we employ to interpret the world around us. These processes are responsible for our everyday awareness; they filter perception, experience, communication – our material worlds. These processes have become a part of our feeling of security and familiarity. Yet they also keep us 'boxed' within the comforts of our conditioning. Any immediate shifting away from these 'comfort patterns' may at first create a sense of disorientation and/or of strangeness. Things in our daily world may become less certain, less 'knowable'. The world around us is constantly in flux, yet persistently being defined and fixed by cognitive conditioning processes. However, these processes can become fluid if approached from the correct forms of perception.

Human consciousness manifests in our daily lives through the cultural lens of our cognitive systems. And these systems are a result of specific, often localized, conditioning. They are often the result of our upbringing, our education, our regional legal

4

systems and cultural 'realities'. Our beliefs too form a part of our cognitive matrix, infused through various faith and/or dogmatic teachings. It is now accepted by modern research that the general person thinks in patterns that become reinforced over the years. After some time a person finds it difficult to adjust to a different cognitive reality, or point of view. Yet everything changes, is subject to change, and must develop (or devolve). In the end, it is all a question of how we perceive the external world *internally*. That is, how matter becomes a part of our mind.

Many commentators have reasoned that modern human life has slipped into a type of existential vacuum, where 'meaning' has become a vague fantasy. Where once life held 'meaning' is now a myth to be told in tales and tall stories. It is a deep shame if this indeed is the case, for 'meaning' is the very essence of creative life. And our intuitive selves should be responsible for divulging meaning to us within the moments we experience. It has been said that:

> each man is questioned by life; and he can only answer to life by *answering for* his own life; to life he can only respond by being responsible.[1]

We are *responsible* then for *how* we think and perceive life. And this responsibility manifests in the world we encounter through our human experiences. What is needed is a revitalization of the sense of human significance: a renewed intention towards creative relations between ourselves and the living cosmos.

If we do not remind ourselves we are likely to forget: *human beings exist in a living universe where consciousness is primary*. And real change has always occurred through the power of focused thought and intention. An individual working alone with the creative force of conscious energies can act upon the world more subtly yet more fully than a battlefield of soldiers or a garrison of uniformed generals.

This short book you now hold in your hands will attempt to explain to you some of the capacities of conscious thinking, and to place this within an historical and cultural context. Also, to remind the reader of those capacities which lie within each person for energetically engaging with the everyday world. It is a testimony to the power of the energies inherent within each of us that humanity has evolved thus far, and continues to evolve toward an unprecedented future. Although we may well have had some help along the way, the future most surely now rests within our hands... or minds!

After all, within our intuitive selves lies the true capacity for magic...

A TALE TO FINISH:

The Magician's Dinner

There was once a Magician who built a house near a large and prosperous village. One day he invited all the people of the village to dinner. 'Before we eat,' he said, 'we have some entertainments.'

Everyone was pleased, and the Magician provided a first-class conjuring show, with rabbits coming out of hats, flags appearing from nowhere, and one thing turning into another. The people were delighted. Then the Magician asked: 'Would you like dinner now, or more entertainments?'

Everyone called for entertainments, for they had never seen anything like it before; at home there was food, but never such excitement as this. So the Magician changed himself into a pigeon, then into a hawk, and finally into a dragon. The people went wild with excitement.

He asked them again, and they wanted more. And they got it. Then he asked them if they wanted to eat, and they said that they did. So the Magician made them feel that they were eating, diverting their attention with a number of tricks, through his magical powers.

The imaginary eating and entertainments went on all night. When it was dawn, some of the people said, 'We must go to work.' So the Magician made those people imagine that they went home, got ready for work, and actually did a day's work.

In short, whenever anyone said that he had to do something, the Magician made him think first that he was going to do it, then, that he had done it and finally that he had come back to the Magician's house.

Finally the Magician had woven such spells over the people of the village that they worked only for him while they thought that they were carrying on with their ordinary lives. Whenever they felt a little restless he made them think that they were back at dinner at his house, and this gave them pleasure and made them forget.

And what happened to the Magician and the people, in the end? Do you know, I cannot tell you, because he is still busily doing it, and the people are still largely under his spell.[1]

One

Creative Forces Throughout History

Humanity has always been inextricably bound up within the laws of the Earth. There was a time too, long ago in human history, when the human 'being' (and the part it played) was viewed as relating to all the laws and activities of the cosmos. This knowledge was taught in the ancient 'mystery' schools where the teachers of the past explained the cosmic aspect of the soul. These centers were the forerunner to our schools/universities today; yet their teachers were like artists/priests combined. Socrates and Plato admitted their initiation in the Mysteries of Eleusis; yet the Eleusinian mysteries were not alone in their role. Mystery schools like hidden fires burned brightly under the canopy of the ancient world: the Orphic Mysteries; the Phrygian Mysteries; the Chaldean and Assyrian Mysteries; the Mysteries of Mithras and Samothrace. Centers of inner wisdom spread from Persia, Babylonia, Greece, and Rome. Yet it seems these were only the seedlings for the parent tree was the Egyptian Mystery School of Isis, a center of esoteric learning that provided nourishment for the inner world of humankind. Or for those who had eyes to see, and ears to hear.

Knowledge was sown into cultural 'carriers' (forms of transmission) such that it would be handed down through myths and legends that are nowadays scattered and yet sadly little understood. The inspired minds of people in the past were occupied more with creative pictures of the world/cosmos and the power to 'communicate' with these conscious, living processes. To lose sight of these relations was to become 'distracted' by worldly things, with the 'fallen world' of materiality. It was the purpose of such *occult* activities to keep alive in the collective memory the spark of 'divine connection', or *source of the spirit*. Such mysteries were sought through the strengthening of deep intuition and refined perceptions.

Deep intuition is sometimes referred to as human imagination (the capacity to manifest rather than to fantasize!). The word *imagination* contains 'magi', the Latin plural of 'magus' (ancient Greek 'magos') which translates into the English 'magian'. Magian survives in the abbreviated form today as *magic* (and as 'magie', the German word for magic). True 'imagination' is part of the sphere of magic. The words of the ancient past held more power; today words are rarely recognized in their connection to occult meanings and the ability to manifest energetic connections. The use of words today is more to manipulate the position of the speaker rather than to elevate.

Thus, the imagination of the aspirant for inner learning was disciplined, trained, and developed. The simplest of exercises was likely to include reviewing each day at its end, to enhance the memory and to 'fix' the experiences and senses of the day. The review would begin backwards and end at the moment of awakening. Such ways were used to stimulate and enhance inner activity; to develop more intensively the forces which radiate through the individual.

These 'creative forces' helped to bind the individual to the larger cosmos as well as to earthly life. Physical relations were not forgotten for they had to be attended to in order to maintain life. Yet a more balanced proportion was maintained between the material (outer) and the inner worlds. Each had its place within the realm of the other. The essence of each gave life force to the other and thus a reciprocal maintenance was established. This reciprocity also played a role in the earthly laws of evolution by producing a channel (humankind) as a vessel for the channeling of creative, evolutionary energies. Such evolutionary laws operate throughout history and are the deeper laws that penetrate all appearances. These are the forces that have operated behind the rise and fall of consecutive societies and civilizations. Great waves of creative, imaginative thought have served as the seeds of many great cultural formations. These seeds have been planted and sown by the creative interventions of conscious forces. The human race has been operating under these laws at all times.

All great interventions of conscious renewal have been part of the ongoing process of human, cultural, and spiritual evolution. True revolutions are not those of physical violence but of radical shifts in perceptions, knowledge, and ultimately the individual and collective consciousness.

Works of art and architecture, edifices of text and textures, have been utilized as tools to educate and prepare humanity for its continued evolution. Such tools function to restructure the world for us, to create an altogether different form of understanding beyond that of the material realm. Ultimately, we can develop a completely different view of the world if we are able to continually transform our cognitive systems. This tells us we are required to shift our perceptual paradigms in line with intensifying evolutionary energies. Whereas in the past the individual would trust in the senses of their interior life, we now largely lie in neglect of the function of inner knowledge and intuition.

Yet operative events have occurred throughout world history with the intention of seeding higher functioning into human consciousness. These events have taken the form of artistic movements; scientific innovations; faith movements; cultural/social revolutions; architecture; fraternities; myths and legends; sporting fixtures, and more. All such operations have served to impact upon the consciousness of humankind, and in a way that prepares the human mind for periods of development and change. One such operation in recent human history can be said to include the early Christian monastic culture which created centers for knowledge storing and transmission. This then developed into the era of the European cathedral building, which resulted in the Abbey Church of Cluny, Chartres, Rheims,

Mont St. Michel, and the guilds of the cathedral builders. This movement was also closely tied to the Crusades and the subsequent rise of chivalric guilds. Following on from this operative period was the emergence of the Renaissance in Florence circa 1450. This artistic and cultural 'happening' was populated by such notable figures as Medici, da Vinci, and other intelligentsia. This influence spread to Cambridge, Oxford, and many other places that subsequently became centers of learning and education.

The second half of the previous millennium was populated with many significant cultural events, including the Reformation, the French Revolution, and various other faith-based and political/state revolutions. Within these many seemingly random occurrences lay the components that acted as the 'technologies' for developing human consciousness. It can be said that the last thousand years of our human history, in particular, has seen the rapid expansion of humankind's information field, and thus increased social-cultural development. It is speculated that the increasing mutation in the collective consciousness of humankind is in line with certain evolutionary necessities. Within this development lie the catalysts for stimulating perceptual capacities that have largely lain dormant within the majority of humankind. Preparation has been necessary through a succession of events that overall form a pattern of mutually reinforcing stimuli aimed at raising humanity's psychic density. Involved here is the expansion of intellect, psychological awareness, development of social exchange, humanitarianism, empathy, and creative capacities. These advances have also sought to once again provide humankind with a link to grander cosmic operations and principles. Part of the requirement, it seems, is a revitalization of the intuitive connection and a greater flow and communion between the interior and exterior realms. Through the greater usage and familiarity of this connection can other latent capacities within humankind come to the fore.

One such event in our world history where a revolution in the imagination occurred was that of the Troubadours. The troubadours brought about a revolution in the way *love* was expressed, thought about, and experienced. It was a time where an interior longing could be expressed externally in a way never articulated before. It thus created the conditions for others to experience and share in these feelings and conscious expressions. The experience of falling in love was deliberately introduced into the cultural stream of human consciousness, and the experience of 'being in love' was given a structure, a vessel, for its growth and evolution. Although the word troubadour is often credited with deriving from the Provençal verb *trobar*, meaning 'to find' or 'to invent', it has been shown that it is more likely to have come from the Arabic root TRB (with the *ador* suffix added).[2] The TRB root suggests a range of words that include a meeting place of friends, a Master, playing the viol, and the idealization of women. The troubadours appeared to encapsulate these meanings in their mysterious gatherings and dissemination of a new consciousness of longing. Courtly love provided a vessel for bridging interior yearning to an exterior expression. Through this channel other courtly endeavors could arise, notably in court chivalry that grew rapidly around the same time. Notably, chivalric ideals were absorbed into literary works such as Chretien de Troyes romantic Arthurian legends and the Holy Grail. Dante's *Divina Commedia* too owes much to this conscious influence. Chivalric orders such as the Knights Templar and others can be seen as having a debt to the troubadour influence. The injection of this deliberate developmental impulse spread rapidly through both mental and physical channels.

By injecting into public consciousness expressions of longing, desire, the unattainable beloved, and chivalric etiquette, later cultural impulses were seeded. From this have arisen codes of conduct, artistic aspirations, architectural monuments, and various other cultural reminders for the human psyche. It can also be said that the modern-day pop song owes a debt to the troubadour influence. Never has the outward expression of a person's love and yearning been so easily achievable to so wide an audience.

Similar cultural artifacts can also be seen to have been operating during the phenomenon that was the Western 1960s. On the surface it seems as if there was a deliberate operation to bring an 'Eastern' body of energy and teachings over to the 'West' during the period around the 1960s. The influx of esoteric teachings and oriental formulations arose suddenly in western Europe and North America at exactly the same time that several 'cultural revolutions' were underway. Although this also led to the rise in 'guru-ism' and Western 'seekers' following touristic Ashram trails, Jalal ad-Din Rumi reminds us that: "False gold only exists because there is such thing as the Real."

Many profound socio-cultural signifiers were seeded during this short period of quite radical change. Many peoples' consciousness and perceptions were altered permanently. Without this preparation it seems less likely there would have been a New Age/Aquarian impulse; the 1987 *Harmonic Convergence*; and the increasing acceptance of transcendental/psychological experiences. The 1960s 'cognitive mutation' laid much of the groundwork for what is coming to the fore at this present time.

Catalytic events have often occurred at times when more rapid social change is required. It may be that such an important period of change is happening today. The upheaval in global changes we are currently witnessing would certainly indicate that circumstances are converging towards some radical shifts. This holds profound implications for our global social systems as well as for humanity.

Throughout history there have been those who have surmised such forces operating behind the façade of cultural change. The playwright George Bernard Shaw once remarked that:

> ...behind events there are evolutionary forces which transcend our ordinary needs and which use individuals for purposes far transcending that of keeping those individuals alive and prosperous and respectable and safe and happy.

It may be that such 'evolutionary forces' that Shaw points to are at an intense stage during the present epoch. If this is the case, then it is crucial that certain cognitive developments are stimulated during this phase. Perhaps it has never been more necessary for a change in the way we *think*. Or rather, how we *perceive* our connections with a conscious, living cosmos. Again, how *we view* determines how *we do*.

And the world that currently holds our attention is a mighty distracter. It has now become a force that pulls our attention outwards to the detriment of our inner cognition. This has proven to be an unhealthy and unbalanced relationship. It may now be due for an overhaul...

A TALE TO FINISH:

Stories

A reputable wise man always taught his students in the form of parables and stories, which they would listen to with real pleasure. However, the students were also sometimes frustrated because they longed for something 'deeper'. The wise man did not care at all about such objections. His answer would always be the same:

'You still have to understand that the shortest distance between man and the truth is a story.'

Two

Signs of Our Times

We are living through very interesting times. Yet unlike the Chinese 'curse' – *May you live in interesting times* – the prevailing and coming years don't need to be to our misfortune. Nevertheless, they will be remarkable. The next twenty years will be so very different from the past twenty years. Rather than living through 'interesting times' we are now entering *momentous times*. The next decade or two will be especially intense, and may prove to be a period of change in social, cultural, and political systems as well as mental and emotional patterns.

If one wishes to consider this astrologically, planet Earth is currently riding through a Uranus-Pluto wave. Uranus brings freedom and innovation (awakening or disruptive), whereas Pluto signifies depths and power (empowering or destroying).[3] These available energies provide the means for profound change as they present a major tipping-point for global civilization. They can be disruptive and destroying, pointing the way towards breakdown; or they can be awakening and empowering, leading the way towards breakthrough. The next twenty years may prove whether human societies succeed in navigating past an upcoming pivotal crossroads.[4] We are collectively entering a period of unprecedented change. And every change has simultaneously required an accompanying change in consciousness – in our *cognitive systems*. This has always been the case. How we respond to, and use, the available energies will be largely a question of our cognitive capacities.

This era of change will heighten existing sensitivities. Current psychological and mental imbalances will be made more prevalent. Similarly, human perception and sensitivity will be intensified and exaggerated. This may require us to adopt a different set of reference points in order to identify with our everyday 'reality'. Decisive actions and insightful vision will have increased impact than at other times. Such influences will reverberate and disseminate more strongly during these heightened moments. This will be a period where so many things will be highlighted, challenged, and tested. In other words, there has never been a more pressing time for conscious *mindfulness*. We have gone as far as we can get with our state of denial as part of a living, vibrant, conscious cosmos. What may be forced upon us will be a 'cleansing of our house', which in itself will be a 'wake-up call'. Situations may arise that call into play different aspects of our being. This is likely to impact our very principles and cherished beliefs. Again, we are being asked to think about *how and what we think* – and *why?*

Looking at the world around us it seems that we are living in a perpetual state of disturbance and upheaval; reinforced by 'rational intelligence' yet not restrained by awareness. It appears that a great deal of complexity is overriding our fundamental and 'simple' basics. This may be an error of perception: it may 'simply' be a question of "the end of our exploring/Will be to arrive where we started/And know the place for the first time."[5]

However, many of us go through life as automatons, barely touching the epidermis of wakefulness. We are often out-of-synch and whistling a wrong tune. We need to shake the sleep from our eyes. It appears that there is too much 'information' but not sufficient 'meaning' in our lives. Many so-called 'civilized' cultures put great store by the collection of information like greedy children. Yet we can be intellectual giants while at the same time being spiritual infants. Great intelligence is often little more than showing an accomplished cerebral dexterity – this can still be *dead intelligence*, as opposed to *living intelligence*. Behind this often lies a lack of engagement with the creative imagination, deep insight, and is replaced with low quantities of conscious awareness. As one celebrated thinker put it:

People today are in danger of drowning in information; but, because they have been taught that information is useful, they are more willing to drown than they need be. If they could handle information, they would not have to drown at all.[6]

The emphasis is often placed upon a one-way processing of information on a daily basis rather than having a living engagement. Modern industrialized society trains us to be consummate data-jugglers, honing our mental agility, while we renege on our conscious awareness. People are in danger of becoming data carriers. Our focus should be less upon the pitcher and more upon the water – less upon the container and more upon the content.

Much of modern life has become an unbalanced distraction. For many it can be said that the world is an 'attention distracter' (AD). For such people, they are truly living in the 21st century **AD** – to the full. We suffer less from an 'attention deficit' but more from 'attention overload' – or rather misplaced attention. The external environment is complete with too much inter-ference and static. There is too much of the glitter-ball and not enough of the homing-call. Too much attention has been placed upon exterior gratifications often at the expense of our inner state. In general, we are in need of transformation; yet a transfor-mation that has a deep focus upon the inner, perceptive realm. Any sort of external, socio-cultural transformation without the accompanying progress in consciousness is in danger of disem-powering us. Our living social matrix is already dependent upon our attachment to external systems and controlling technologies. Such exterior loyalties where we give away our inner authority only serve to further emasculate ourselves in the face of our own great human adventure. Sadly, this relationship all too easily perpetuates itself. It has been remarked that:

One shouldn't worry about taking pictures or making tape

recordings. Those are superfluities of sedate lives. One should worry about the spirit, which is always receding.[7]

At the same time it is often assumed that something which is transcendental or 'spiritual' must be far off or complicated. This is nothing more than a lack of knowledge from those least qualified to judge. What lies within is only 'far off' in a direction a person does not comprehend.

Another misconception, and one that is important to the realm of the creative imagination, is that of original thinking. Nothing is original, although each thought or event may seem unique to our set of experiences. Everything has gone before, and every possibility exists in potential. Further, each of us possesses the capacity and potential to bring into existence, or manifest, developing awareness. It is therefore important how we deal with each experience, event, situation(s), and circumstances. We create meaning not by what *happens to us*, but rather how *we respond* to our circumstances. It can also be stated that there are no original thoughts or words; what exists are unique ways of making the unknown known – or rather, manifesting that which is not yet manifest. Each of us is already that 'original element' that no originality can supersede. At the same time we each have the capacity to express life through our own interpretations. We have at our disposal the power of creative intention to manifest our every moment as a meaningful experience. Each time we do this we open up the meaningful possibilities and potentials of our future. Psychologist Viktor Frankl expressed this as:

…man's main concern is not to gain pleasure or to avoid pain but rather to see a meaning in his life. That is why man is even ready to suffer, on the condition, to be sure, that his suffering has a meaning.[8]

Here, importance is being given to those aspects of life that are the potentialities. Nietzsche rather elegantly summed this up by saying: "He who has a *why* to live for can bear almost any *how*." It is up to each one of us, in a balanced way, to capture the sense of life's potentialities – even in disruptive periods.

We create our futures – for good or for bad – within each 'present moment' through our active experiences. Our internal selves are involved at each step of the way within these experiential moments. Yet nothing in this world is for free: we must earn what we learn. The question is – do we ever use it? A modern rewriting of an old proverb states that:

Anyone can see that an ass laden with books remains a donkey. A human being laden with the undigested results of a tussle with thoughts and books, however, still passes for wise.[9]

It is the *digestion* of life's events and experiences that has the capacity for meaning. Even when some 'grander sense' in a person's acts cannot be perceived, a person should still act *as if* there is meaning in everything they do. This is the true mode of human participation within an energetic living environment. It should be remembered that 'meaning' also operates beyond a person's comprehension and scope of understanding. In varying degrees 'meaning' operates within each person's sphere of personal affect and influence. Through conscious intent a person can become more aware of how meaningful action comes into play.

Being more aware as a person does not confer parapsychological powers onto you (an ESP Guru), nor does it require an Eastern pilgrimage. It first asks that you listen to yourself. It then requires that you take great care in how you *listen and interpret* the external world. It is not a practice that requires one to be skinny and ascetic. Nor need it be mystical or hysterical. In fact, it is more often humorous and straightforward: more science than superstition. Don't get confused with mystic-babble: 'illumination of the elect' may be nothing more than a rich person turning on their light bulb.

For many people the linkage between the exterior and interior worlds still remains murky and fuzzy. Most daily perceptions and interpretations (the cultural 'cognitive system') remain within the confines of arranged parameters. Intellectual thought is also constricted by layers of conditioning and operates largely mechanically. Instances of authentic creative thought and behavior are more suspected than made openly. Over historical time there has been a diminishing in the 'magic' of our collective creative imagination. As children we possessed this gift; yet being so powerful it had to be 'educated' out of us. We have been left stripped from childhood of our inheritance. Our social institutions have literally stolen the white rabbit and traded it for sawdust. Yet within each of us we have intuited these remnants of our hidden resources. It is the case that we have generally lacked the knowledge to access and to activate them once again. It is for this reason that operations of creative imagination, such as the troubadours, have been active within periods of human history. And it seems likely that opportunities now exist for rapid and radical shifts of consciousness.

However, under present social conditions the lines between what is deemed normal ('sanity') and abnormal ('insanity') have become increasingly blurred. Behaviors deemed 'sane' and 'insane' function as cultural classifications that help to perpetuate what are accepted norms and rules. A question to ask ourselves is: if our whole society were insane, would we know it?

The stimulation of certain cognitive and creative faculties does require, however, that a person maintains authentic power over themselves. That is, shielded from the bombardment of petty realities and the psychic abuse of petty people. Part of the process begins by understanding how much 'wrong thinking' we perpetuate in regard to everything we claim as our own: our thoughts, views, beliefs, tastes, habits. In actual fact so much of our 'baggage' is formed through imitation or from our cultural patterns of conditioning. An old proverb says that: "They that drink of the old wine have no place for the new."

Our 'old wine' has been provided by our social constructs. And while they may vary according to time, place, and people, they all follow some fundamental basics. In brief, they operate to create shared cognitive systems. It is to the subject of how we gained our shared cognitive systems that I now turn.

A TALE TO FINISH:

Madness

There was once a wise and powerful king who ruled in a remote city of a far kingdom. And the king was feared for both his might and his love of wisdom. At the heart of the city was a well whose water was cool and crystalline, and all the inhabitants drank from this well, even the king and his courtiers, because there was no other well in the city. One night, while everyone was asleep, a witch entered the city and poured seven drops of a strange liquid into the well, and said:

'From now on, anyone who drinks this water will go crazy'

The next morning all the inhabitants drank the water from the well, except the king and his lord chamberlain, and very soon everyone went mad, as the witch had foretold. During that day, all people went through the narrow streets and public places whispering to each other:

'The king is mad. Our king and his lord chamberlain have lost their reason. Naturally, we can not be ruled by a mad king. We must dethrone him!'

That night, the king ordered a golden cup of water from the well to be brought to him. And when they brought the cup the king and his lord chamberlain drank heavily from it. Soon after that there was great rejoicing in that distant city of a far kingdom because the king and his lord chamberlain had regained their reason.

Three

Our Cognitive Systems

The influential polymath Ludwig von Bertalanffy wrote that:

> ...training, education, and human life in general are essentially responses to outside conditions: beginning in early childhood with toilet training and other manipulations whereby socially acceptable behavior is gratified and undesirable behavior blocked; continuing with education, which is best carried through according to Skinnerian principles of reinforcement of correct responses and by means of teaching machines and ending in adult man in an affluent society which makes everybody happy, conditioning him, in a strictly scientific manner, by the mass media to be a perfect consumer—that is, an automaton properly answering in the ways prescribed by the industrial-military-political establishment.[10]

With few rare exceptions all people are brought up within culturally-defined environments. The dominating social milieu attempts to offer a variety of accepted socio-cultural norms of thought and behavior. These operate, for example, through religion; science; education; entertainment; family; language and emotions; longing and doubt; happiness and fear; safety and security (identity and belonging); well-being and materialism. It can be said that such prevailing conditions create forms of submersion and submission. Once ingrained, the person is liable to perpetuate such traits believing them to have been obtained through 'free thought'. In the end, we reinforce beliefs that have grown into us, accepting and defending them as our own. Of course, we only 'believe' those things that we want, or that fit within our perceptual paradigms. And we wish to support the investment we have made in 'our beliefs'. For example, a person who likes the music of Leonard Cohen will pay to go to a Leonard Cohen concert but may not pay to see Madonna. Similarly, a person will 'vote' for positive online reviews of a book they themselves like but will likely not vote for the disagreeable reviews. Thus, people seek out and promote those activities and experiences that serve to reinforce and validate their own beliefs. People rarely seek out those experiences that will actively challenge their perceptions and thus create uncertainty and/or doubt. How many far-right conservatives would spend time reading the latest communist newsletter? Yet the fixed idea is the enemy of free thinking.

It has been remarked that the person who gets along best in life is usually the one who displays perfect submission to the norms of the multitude. To attempt to live according to other than the 'norm' of accepted paradigms has usually led to difficulties and certain degrees of estrangement. It can be said, especially in these current times, that leadership increasingly belongs to the mediocre. And whereas the famous edict of the temple of Delphi stated 'Know Thyself', such ideals have been eroded in subsequent generations. Such ancient temples have been replaced by the edifices of education, religion, law, and politics. Certain capacities of the individual have become submerged by a cultural pressure of surrender. Many people may well be able to relate to this situation, yet fewer will have been aware of its steady presence in their lives. The impact is gradual rather than sudden. Since social conditioning serves to strengthen one's sense of acceptance and belonging, soon the influence of the collective mind reinforces and modifies most physical, mental, and emotional behavior. Thus, the person who becomes deemed most socially valuable is often that person who has demonstrated their ability to adopt (and adapt to) consensual patterns. Such patterning often begins very early in a child's life and is usually the formative impacts and experiences.

Indoctrination during childhood generally goes through several stages. The first stage has been named 'Limited Perceptions' and is where the child comes to believe certain things about the world around them because the child doesn't see anything else. These initial belief sets are then reinforced by stage two. This stage is named 'Perceptual Set' whereby the child's attention is drawn to those 'sets' that reinforce the current programmed patterns.[11] For example, when you buy a new car you suddenly see many of them on the road whereas before you didn't notice them. Thus, initial impressions are reinforced and further cemented. And the human 'social animal' is prone to clinging stubbornly to first impressions, even when they are contradicted by later information (known as the 'primacy affect'). These processes of early indoctrination might be open to later reevaluation if it were not for continuing sets of social reinforcement. Many aspects of society are set up to provide each person with successive impacts of like-minded conditioning. For example, the area where a child lives will influence which school they go to and the kind of children they meet and hang around with. This will have an influence on the type of academic progress they make. And all through these early years of schooling the child will likely meet like-minded others who will support their early programming and worldview. On top of this the child will be subject to those beliefs that have been imposed by the parents. These beliefs provide a structure to filter and create a worldview and will be used to interpret all subsequent experiences. The combined effects of these two processes – early childhood indoctrination and parental socialization – are often successful in conditioning an individual to a specific 'cognitive and perceptual reality'. This in turn may create and strengthen a dependence upon any given belief system(s). The unconscious indoctrination of childhood is liable to leave a person open to further layers of conditioning and indoctrination. It is thus the

Breaking The Spell ~ An Exploration of Human Perception

case that:

> ...most of us are indoctrinated throughout our lives, often
> without knowing it. Beliefs almost 'grow' into us. They are
> then sustained and protected, usually unconsciously, by the
> physiological and psychological processes of perception.[12]

By covering oneself with such patterned behavior the person has, often unknowingly, created many layers of conditioning upon their instinctual selves. Inner 'senses' are softened and often silenced through these processes. In the end, conscience may be the only valve still operating within a person. Conscience can function as a channel that bridges a person's external selves and their interior sense of awareness. Yet conscience has a morass of beliefs to wade through, all vying for pole position.

The beliefs that a person holds are further strengthened by not being called into question. And when beliefs are never, or rarely, questioned it is easier for a person to forget why they hold them. It should be remembered that beliefs are not facts: a belief is a 'belief' because it is neither knowledge, nor truth. It is a conviction of faith – a thought-form backed by emotional attachment. Knowing why a person holds a particular belief will not necessary bring knowledge onto the subject. When examined many beliefs are found to result from indoctrination through various processes, such as emotional language and heavily-laden associations. Examples here include love of country (patriotism; nationalism); love of god; love of family and tribe; love of principles and a sense of moral self. For many of these beliefs a whole group of people – even a nation – may sacrifice much in defense of shared emotional investment. And if a majority of people share the same belief(s) then it is unlikely they will be called into question. To do so could result in a person exhibiting 'abnormal' behavior. What actually passes for 'normal' behavior is that which adjusts to the biological and psychological

26

collective. To stand apart from mass behavior is often considered 'abnormal'. Yet rather than these terms being questioned they are accepted as given. Perhaps it would be better to ask: 'what is optimal human behavior?'

Many beliefs and associated behavior patterns are covert expressions of social conformity. From childhood we have been conditioned to adopt behavioral positions that bring rewards of love and attention from our parents. Some of these programs continue with us into adulthood such that people join different causes and/or ideologies to fulfill a need to belong. The need to be accepted and receive attention is often the greater cause, making the ideological cause superficial. Without realizing it a person is often more likely to desire a sense of 'social belonging' which they may have been denied elsewhere (see Appendix).[13] Within this milieu a person is more likely to be influenced to say and do the same as others around them:

> The need to be one with a group, to have group approval and therefore social approval, means that individuals will very often change their attitudes *themselves,* to fit with the norm, instead of having to be persuaded... the passive power exerted by social norms is all the stronger than overt power because it is bowed to unconsciously.[14]

Such is the powerful pull of social conformity. The danger here is that in such environments a person is more likely to give away their personal responsibility than act upon it. A group more generally exhibits a lack of responsibility on the part of its members since each person thinks that the overall responsibility can be shared. Since there is no individual blame to be accrued, a person tends to relinquish their own personal responsibility. The result is that each person reinforces the other's inertia. Thus, non-action actually becomes the accepted norm within the group. This inertia is then reinforced and validated, often through personal rationalization, since so much has been invested in the group. To be wrong could inflict much angst upon an individual; it is therefore better to rationalize one's actions as correct.

These processes of indoctrination are rife within many 'civilized' societies. It is in this way that cognitive systems beneficial to a particular society are created and sustained. Part of this system entails the deliberate programming of obedience to authority figures.[ii] A child from a young age is exposed first to parents, then to school teachers; next to uniformed civil servants; and finally to bosses. An individual is thus trained how to operate, and respond correctly, within the established hierarchical social system. This creates the 'belief' that a person is never totally free in their behavior; they are almost always under the authority of someone above them who influences events. Paradoxically, many people insist to themselves that they have personal freedom, yet externally they fear exhibiting 'too much' freedom. It has been found that people who conform most are likely to have the least tolerance for uncertainty and ambiguity. Social conformity has thus inculcated a feeling of safety: belonging is a safe haven from where a person is protected. To be submerged in the mass makes people feel normal: no one is staring at them. Yet such emotions – of comfort and dis-comfort – are often programs socially conditioned from birth. These processes form our cognitive systems and arrange how we perceive the world around us. Much of our 'human behavior' thus stems from the influences that have shaped us. We are, after all, social animals. Yet what is often not realized is the degree to which these social forces are deliberately constructed in order to mold and govern a collective mass. Our cognitive knowledge systems are thus frequently lacking in genuine stimuli.

The physical 'reality' is that we enroll in systems of imitation through which we are trained to memorize information which is passed as knowledge. This information is then reinforced through socio-cultural institutions, making it appear as true. Even that which is labeled as 'common knowledge' may not be what it claims to be: "The more you look at 'common knowledge', the more you realize that it is more likely to be common than it is to be knowledge. No real knowledge is common."[15]

Alternative systems of thought are often labeled as subversive and subject to human acts of modification and/or dismissal. In this manner specific physical, mental, and emotional patterns are engrained, reinforced, and modulated by human institutions. Human beings are perceivers, yet the world that we perceive is an illusion. This illusion has been reinforced from birth to adulthood. This is the 'reality' that human reason wants to sustain and validate. It is also the 'reality' that many fight to defend and to disseminate.

In the end, we can say that culture is, to a large degree, a prefabrication that serves interests not always within the individual's favor. The cacophony of our consumer-led societies acts like whale calls that lull us into sleep. Our modern-age AD ('Attention Distracter') serves to annul the anxieties that we manifest by our common assent to a pacifying society.

The pacification of human creativity and vital energy is aided by the constant bombardment of audiovisual stimuli. These continual impacts powerfully influence the human psyche. Although on the one hand they create fascination within complex lives, they also generate trancelike states. These states are then maintained and reinforced between the individual and their environment through constant processes of feedback. It is a cycle from which it is hard to break away and to detach from. It can be said that culture "encages, limits, obliges, impels, hypnotizes, and possesses the individual *with irresistible* power, *shaping him in* accordance with one single pattern."[16] This 'single pattern' involves the great subtlety of imitation.

People serve the external world in a way that vastly absorbs their vital energy. The collective energy of the cultural consciousness is thus imprinted by reinforcing energy patterns. In other words, cognitive conditioning is maintained and supported by the conscious energy that is radiated by the masses. This conscious energy actually imposes a 'vibratory pattern' upon an individual which then impels them to act according to its particular vibration.

The human environment is constantly irradiated with the nervous energy of dissonance and static. The airwaves are a sea of discord, grating with the hum of artificial signals. The human spectrum in which a person functions is now an electromagnetic chamber. The human species has altered its electromagnetic background so drastically that "the density of radio waves around us now is 100 million or 200 million times the natural level reaching us from the sun."[17] It can be said that the greatest polluting element in the Earth's environment during our present era is the rapid growth in electromagnetic fields. These are caused by such sources as power lines, satellites, and mobile phones. Those in the West especially live in a world swamped by electrical appliances. The rapid rise in mobile phone usage worldwide has contributed significantly to our exposure to electromagnetic energy above and beyond our normal limits. It has been said that:

> ...life in a mechanized, industrialized, digitalized environment has a deadening effect on our mental processes. The concrete, the plastic, the metal, the electrical impulses bouncing off the screen become internalized, resulting in a sterile wasteland that does not regenerate itself.[18]

And within this electromagnetic distraction the inner creative energies become capped and submerged in the face of progressive dehumanization. Perhaps within the matrixes of noise and conditioning lurks the fear of freedom?

Social and cultural necessities include the need for a person's dependency. Without such 'conditioned loyalty' a nation/state/region loses its regenerative capacity. In this context, freedom causes concerns for social/state institutions. Thus, the habit of obedience is factored into conditioning processes. This engrained obedience fixes perceptual patterns that famously resist paradigm change. The battlefield for such change occurs between a person's inner self and exterior institutions. This conflict creates a form of cognitive dissonance that is common in cultures of obedience. Long periods of dependency and protection serve to cultivate a person's need for belonging. This biological and psychological conditioning has become an inherent part of human culture. Inward vulnerability is thus compensated by attaching to, or giving away responsibility to, an external power. Modern society is thus constructed in a way that seemingly bestows independence upon the individual while simultaneously binding them to external restraints. Over time this relationship functions to weaken a person's reliance upon their inner realms and upon their own flashes of intuition. The habit of obedience becomes an unseen tether that quells the inner need for self-awareness. In this way 'freedom' becomes a fasci-nation when it relates to powers outside of an individual.[19] Yet it blinds people to the condition of their own inner restraints. The exterior realm thus becomes the only sphere of influence and importance within a person's life. The 'Master' exists as physical flesh and blood, concrete and plastic, demanding servitude.

All too easily we give our power away. It is as if our own internal power is something we cannot use, or do not know how to use. Yet by giving power away a person is attracting external power to be used against them. It is as if a person is signaling their submission. Naturally, such offers attract distasteful buyers. It is so easy to become a prey to external authorities that sap our vital energies. This only furthers the illusion that a person exists as a self-willing individual. And this illusion is often maintained through our incessant inner talking. We often talk to ourselves incessantly about the world. In this way the world we experience daily is maintained by our internal talk. A person thus renews and reinforces the external realm that is likely to be different from how it is *actually* perceived. Yet such inner perceptions are overridden by an incessant superficial internal talk. And we keep on repeating the same internal talk over and over like a nursery rhyme. It is as if we fear a vacuum inside, a silent space. Our conditioned 'reality' continues to revolve external to us because we fuel it by our internal chatter. And so it is the case that the world we experience on a daily basis is a reflection of the nature of our inner talk. We project ourselves upon the external environment, as if viewing a mirror that chatters deep through us.

We are never allowed to forget that we are all physical human creatures. Thus, each person faces a physical struggle as well as a mental, spiritual, and emotional one. Little do we realize what kind of power lies within each of us. And everybody has enough personal power for something.

Let us be reminded that the future is open. And in these unfolding times it is important that the future not be about categorization, competition, or colonization. Rather, it is about creation, collaboration, and consciousness. And in order to create, we must first break our own spell.

A TALE TO FINISH:

The Apple of Understanding

The teacher always told a parable at the end of each class, but not all the listeners would understand the meaning of it. One day one of them confronted the teacher and said:

- You tell us stories but do not explain the meaning to us.

The teacher apologized for this and then continued by saying:

- Let me recompense you by offering you a juicy apple.
- Thank you master, the disciple replied flattered.
- First, I would like to peel this apple myself, would I allow it?
- Yes, thank you very much, replied the disciple.
- Since I already have a knife in my hand, let me take advantage of this and cut the apple into pieces so it will be more comfortable for you to eat.
- Thank you teacher, I hope it is not too much trouble?
- Not at all, I just want to please you. Also, allow me to chew it before to make it easier for you to swallow.
- No teacher!, don't do that! shrieked the surprised student.

The teacher paused and said:

- If I explain the meaning of each parable .... it would be like feeding you a fruit chewed. You yourself have to find and savor its exquisite flavor.

Four

Breaking the Spell

Consensus reality is a bewitching spell. It fascinates and beguiles. Tolstoy wrote that "Truth, like gold, is to be obtained not by its growth, but by washing away from it all that is not gold." By washing our awareness we may help to clean the lens of our perception. We can revitalize our energies by the mere act of forming new 'attentions'. The new currency here is not fiat money but conscious awareness. And it buys a lot more too. As the aphorism goes – *'Take what you want says God, but pay for it'*. Nothing in our world is for free. Even the act of changing one's thinking patterns comes at a price. Yet it should be remembered that all genuine transactions are reciprocal. With real effort comes reward. However, real effort is best practiced when absent from the need or desire for reward.

Most social systems operate through mechanisms of encouragement and reward (the carrot and the stick). Again, such distractions serve to draw the attention outside of oneself, as opposed to nurturing the intention within. Our 'civilized' societies have directed attention away from the need for an individual to act authentically: that is, driven not by externally motivated desires but from genuine internal impulses. This necessitates the formation of disciplined *intention*. What this *intention* involves is the capacity to direct oneself in life without imitation or need for recognition and approval. The cultivation of inner intention can itself lead to knowing 'right action'. This is when *conscience* is operating in balance with intuition and the creative imagination of a person's interior life. Outward actions appear as if directed by a form of conscience, and feel 'right'. When conscience and genuine inner feeling (the 'gut feeling') are operating together there is an *intention* that exists which is neither thought, nor wish, nor an object. It is an *intention* that can override the thoughts of conditioning. It creates a form of internal strength and control that can resist the daily barrage of social memes and manipulative impacts. It gives a person the power to resist subtle forms of social control. However, power is not the force we have over others but rather the force we have within ourselves. It is through this force that a person is able to manifest 'sincere intent' through their actions and behavior. It is worth recalling here a saying attributed to Sayedna Ali who stated: "The rights that others have over you – remember them. The rights that you have over others – forget them."

It will be necessary during the years ahead of socio-cultural change that our intentions also connect with the accompanying 'cognitive shift'. What we are currently passing through is another revolution in human consciousness. It is a time to be open to changing the rigidity of one's thoughts, beliefs, and 'sacred' attachments. What enslaves a person is that which holds their attention externally. There is an oral anecdote about the Sufi mystic Rabia Al-Adawiya who when asked by a friend on a beautiful spring morning to come outside of the house to see the bounteous works of God, she replied: "Come you inside that you may behold their Maker. Contemplation of the Maker has turned me aside from what He has made." Like Rabia's friend the majority of us are focused on the secondary in a way that occupies us totally. It is a consuming relationship, and one that requires all our available energies. It is in this manner that many mystics have referred to humanity as being 'asleep'.

To 'awaken' the faculties of perception and creative vision calls into being a whole new cognitive system; a reassembling of how our physical senses interpret the world around us. It calls for mental concentration that can replace a person's old conditioned terms of reference for new terms of reference which are more positive and useful. These new terms of reference should form part of a mental discipline. If people could be more aware of the ways in which they think and react – to observe their responses – they could create their own inner strengths. Such mental discipline also refers to a quality of action. To strengthen one's inner life does not infer inner retreat every second of every day; it requires a balance (as discussed in Chapter Six). It involves knowing when to include and when to exclude. With lesser energy a person can often feel helpless in the face of external influences and impacts. It is necessary to hold some disciplinary power over those things/people/events that we wish to either include or exclude from the realm of our daily world. In other words, we need to rearrange our storage of experiences. When an encounter/event/impact is received we should immediately ask ourselves as to its nature and whether it is of benefit to us. The question of conscious-level storage is sometimes more of a question of what to throw away. Failure to activate this filtering only adds to our loss of internal power and discipline. From this a person can become weaker within their lives, pushed around by the influence of arbitrary forces. By being an independent presence in the world we are being asked to assume responsibility for this gift. The average person far too often acts on their thoughts and desires without taking responsibility for them. We need to assume the responsibility of our presence in the world: in this time, now, and through each moment and encounter.

By taking responsibility in this way we make each moment and encounter our own. By not taking such responsibility we let events drift away from us or become powerless to defend against their disruptive influence. In each moment there exists the opportunity for the reciprocal exchange of energies; such exchanges are the binds that serve to arrange a person's life. Creative inner discipline allows a person to grab onto more things in life. Life is shorter than we may realize; or rather, when we eventually realize how short life can be, it's often too late. This is nicely indicated by the following story:

A miser had accumulated, by effort, trade and lending, three hundred thousand dinars. He had lands and buildings, and all kinds of wealth. He then decided that he would spend a year in enjoyment, living comfortably, and then decide as what his future should be.

But, almost as soon as he had stopped amassing money the Angel of Death appeared before him, to take his life away.

The miser tried, by every argument which he could muster, to dissuade the Angel, who seemed, however, adamant. Then the man said: "Grant me but three more days and I will give you one-third of my possessions."

The angel refused, and pulled again at the miser's life, tugging to take it away. Then the man said:

"If you only allow me two more days on Earth, I will give you two hundred thousand dinars from my store." But the Angel would not listen to him. And the Angel even refused to give the man a solitary extra day for all his three hundred thousand pieces. The miser then said:

"Please, then, give me just time enough to write one little thing down."

This time the Angel allowed him this single concession, and the man wrote, with his own blood:

Man, make use of your life. I could not buy one hour for three hundred thousand dinars. Make sure that you realize the value of your time.[20]

Time often appears to speed up for an individual as experiences accumulate. Inner awareness can be functional here by arranging how each moment is consciously stored and recreated (see Chapter Five). We have the capacity to embellish our lives through how we perceive and interpret our encounters. And when a person's life is seen within the grander cosmos, it appears as but a speck in time. So it becomes important that a person aims to live through qualitative time – a life of *Kairos*.

Kairos, to the ancient Greeks, was the god of the 'fleeting moment' that presented a passing favorable opportunity within the fate of Man. So *Kairos* time represents living within the state of the *right and opportune moment.* Within such states the human being is more open to connecting events, circumstances, and life's flows. In fact, many people have witnessed incredible 'coincidences' when in certain states of *flow* and qualitative time.[21] Such moments must be seized upon before they are gone, perhaps forever. Within this qualitative state a person is more likely to be able to adapt to changing circumstances and be more open to possibilities. These present times, in fact, demand the qualities of experiencing *Kairos* time in a way that linearity is replaced by *entanglement.* In what has been described as the 'Quantum Age' our modern sciences are finally reconnecting with the ancient knowledge of universal connectedness.

All too often we assume that an event occurs as if it existed separately within a vacuum. In actuality, all events are interconnected and woven with all other events. Our human actions are always prompted by a whole range of events rather than a single cause. Likewise, any action that a person performs is not an isolated event. Each and every action has consequences; many of which are beyond our knowing. Similarly, situations are often changed by events which seemingly have no connecting relevance. By being more internally connected to the external flow of events a person begins to shift from viewing impacts and happenings in a regular linear and limited way. In *Kairos* time, each breath is not counted, but tasted. Taste remains where numbers fade:

Golden Moments

To enjoy them while you can
In the time that you are in
For that very moment
That may not begin again.

They are there to be absorbed
Like the smell from passing skin,
Not to be ignored
For fear of hesitancy within.
In life, moments seek, but do not return.
Golden Moments must always burn.[22]

A person acts as part of the world, yet simultaneously as a contribution within a much grander whole. Sometimes we can do little more than to treat the world as a continuing mystery – as something incomprehensible that at times reveals comprehensible secrets. In this way we can never reach the end, or cease to be enthralled.

Within the comprehensive flow of the incomprehensible lies our ideas of ourselves. When at certain times we are able to 'act' – to do and accomplish things – when before we couldn't, what has changed is the idea we hold of ourselves internally. This internal image that we hold becomes the marker of our ability and capacity *to do* and *to be*. This is the creative perceptual space a person exists within. This is the realm of our deep human creative vision. We may have to change our ideas of our 'selves' in order to catalyze a shift in our cognitive apparatus. For example, with a 'fixed' sense of self a person may react to obstacles by meeting them head-on. This abrasive style is often a way of manifesting one's sense of self-importance. Yet often a more suitable way to navigate through life is not by meeting obstacles head-on but by maneuvering around them as if they were obstacles of less importance. One of these 'maneuvers' is to act without expectation of reward, and to have no expectations from other people. This positioning creates a healthy kind of detachment: a space which can be filled with a more disciplined conscious awareness.

Another 'maneuver' is the rearrangement of internal components. In other words, the shifting of priority of various internal components such as ego; self-importance; responsibility; self-pity; action and inaction; judgment. We often cling to these components in inappropriate degrees. For example, we need to be careful about giving too much priority and importance to our ordinary assessments. Our assessments and forms of judgment are, as already discussed, largely a creation of external social conditioning. As such, they are often culturally and regionally biased. Therefore, we should not be so quick to look at and judge phenomena. When we begin to change these individual aspects of ourselves we start to shift our whole being. This is because a person functions as a systemic whole. So when one part or aspect is changed the whole inner arrangement shifts its pattern. New relations can be formed within a person by making a small change at a time. We should not forget that: "We do have the power to change, but we must change to have the power."[23]

The aim of this brief chapter is to introduce the idea that a person's 'cultural spell' can be broken. New and creative perceptions, thought patterns and behavior can be brought into focus. In a way, we need to 'learn how to learn'. And we need to refresh our sense of self, our convictions and beliefs – even our thoughts. Most of the time we assume we have a stable consciousness. Yet in actuality a person is at the mercy of inner and outer impacts. As such, behavior will vary with emotional states that are affected by unseen forces. All too often a life ends up as an unconscious struggle through a myriad of impacts. What can actually slow this human drama down is disciplined awareness – a fixing (concentrating) of perception. And it is our cognitive systems that interpret and filter our external perceptions. The link between a person's interior realms and the exterior physical world – the perceptual bridge – needs to be polished. Yet the everyday world serves to numb and dumb down our energetic connecting links and creative capacities. Revitalizing these energetic and creative capacities is thus about managing one's energy; being vigilant with oneself; and learning to step away.

I now turn to the following chapters in order to discuss these subjects in greater depth.

A TALE TO FINISH:

Renunciation

After reaching old age, and after a home life of many joys and sorrows, a husband and wife decided to renounce the worldly life and devote the rest of their time to meditation and pilgrimage to the most sacred shrines.

One time, en route to a Himalayan temple, the husband saw on the path in front of him a fabulous diamond. Very quickly, he placed one foot on the jewel to hide it, thinking that if his wife saw it then perhaps a sense of greed would arise in her that could contaminate her mind and delay her mystical evolution. Yet the wife, discovering the ruse of her husband, said in a fair and gentle voice:

'Dear, I would like to know how you have renounced the world if you still make a distinction between diamond and dust.'

Five

Managing One's Energy

We should remind ourselves again about what is the underlying principle of all life: *Everything Is Mind*. All life manifests within a mind-before-matter universe – that is, a conscious universe. As the Hermetic dictum states: *The Universe is Mental*.[24] Our cosmos resonates with energy that is conscious, dynamic and creative. Both the material and the non-material energetic forces operating within the universe are constantly in states of becoming. They represent the unfinished creative energies of change and transformation. In this sense, nothing really 'is' as all and everything fluctuates. The early Greek philosopher Heraclitus emphasized the nature of universal flux and flow: *"There is nothing permanent except change"*; *"All is flux, nothing stays still."* The 'reality' of creation suggests that there is nothing which is not in permanent flux. Change is how life endures. All forces are in continual action and reaction; inflow and outflow; attraction and repulsion. Behind these continual flows is the presence of *Mind*.

Human beings are organisms that both filter and create energy; and through this relation with energy we hold the capacity to alter our sense and perception(s) of our immediate environment. In other words, we exist in a 'sense' environment where our energy fields operate as tactile tentacles. We have the capacity to 'feel' our reality, which then gets filtered through our physical sense apparatus. Since all is energy we need to manage the interactions between interior and exterior energy fields/flows. By learning how to 'free-up' energy a person is then able to save some energy from daily usage and wastage. This stored energy can then be used for a person's own focused intentions and awareness. Without this discipline a person is more vulnerable to the backward and forward swing of pendulum-like forces:

> The masses of people are carried along, obedient to
> environment; the wills and desires of others stronger than
> themselves; heredity; suggestion; and other outward causes
> moving them about like pawns on the Chessboard of Life.[25]

Energy is a material quantity. As such it needs to be considered in terms of its quantitative value. A person has the capacity (and/or access) to only so much energy in their lifetime. Energy should be thus viewed not as a limitless resource but as an endowment. Too many people too much of the time spend energy needlessly on unnecessary and unpleasant emotions. Energy gets used up on expectations, mood swings, nervousness, irritability, wrong imagination, negative thoughts/ intentions, and self-pity.

Desires and misplaced attention are a primary way of wasting this quantitative energy. The fanciful desires that enter us from the world around – our exterior 'social carnival' - can distract and sap our energies. If we could but form small specific goals within our everyday life, and achieve them, this would create more permanent energy within us. To *aim and to achieve* is an energy-fixing exercise. Begin with small aims that are realizable before moving onto larger goals. Allow these aims to be formed not from want but from need. To know what one needs is a higher form of thinking than by being influenced by wants. *To need enough, and want little enough* is a dictum worth following.

The ancient Hermetic art of mental transmutation involved the practice of changing and transforming mental states and conditions. It is both a high art and an everyday practical possibility. A helpful formulation is *Energy Retention, Energy Intention*. A person should aim to store and retain as much personal energy as possible. This personal energy can then be made available for physical aims and achievements through focused intention. A lack of a conscious aim within life goes hand in hand with unfocused and undisciplined interior energy. It is a basic fact of our lives that we give away our energy too easily. It is thus necessary to save, store, and manage one's personal energy: even if for the primary reason that a person needs enough personal energy for self-evolution.

It can be said that most 'unconscious' actions waste energy and that it is conscious action which stores and retains energy. To manage one's energy then requires that we become more conscious over the reciprocation of energies – mentally, physically, and emotionally. Energy is thus lost through unnecessary physical/muscular exertion; unfocused mental exertions and daydreaming; and emotional nervousness or stress.

The picture may be clearer if we consider one of the functions of the human being is to assist in the movement of energies. Humans are agents of transmission – for themselves, for people around them, and for their environment. It can be said that humans both individually and collectively operate as a 'movement of energies'. The human body is like a biological battery – it accumulates, develops, and distributes energies. As such it is necessary for a person to be in harmonious relations with their interactions: with people, situations, emotions, and physical posturing. These concepts are not new; in fact they form a basis of our everyday world. People often talk of sensing 'bad vibes' between people or even in a place. When something just doesn't 'feel right' we need to trust these instinctual signs. It is our responsibility (to our 'selves' and to our energy) to find and nurture right alignments. For example, when in the presence of some people we may recognize that we always have a feeling of being drained of energy. It is as if these people were sucking the energy away from us. In these circumstances we can refer to such people as 'psychic vampires'. Not because they are necessarily evil, dangerous, or denizens of the night. It is because their energy alignments are such that they 'pull in' the energy around them. The reasons for this are various, yet the outcome invariably the same. If it is not your function to 'feed them', then move away – just don't entertain their energy. In a mind-before-matter universe everything is a construction of energy:

> The *human form* is a conglomerate of energy fields which exists in the universe, and which is related exclusively to human beings. Shamans call it the *human form* because those energy fields have been bent and contorted by a lifetime of habits and misuse.[26]

The interior health of the human can be related to the 'shape and form' of one's energy body. Since the universe is *mental* the human body is thus responsive also to our thoughts and their emanations. This creates the need for disciplining one's mental, emotional, and physical states.

All mental processes – all thoughts, intentions, desires and Will – manifest as vibrations. The quality of a person's vibrations will be relative to their mental state and condition. Negative mental states will be accompanied by discordant vibrations. Some of these vibrations will remain within the energy of the person's body, affecting them physically; while the remainder will resonate through the exterior environment. Just as in the vibration of musical sounds, a person's vibration affects the people around them by a form of 'induction'. In simpler terms, everything is in resonance with every other thing. Every thought we have, every act we perform has its direct and indirect results through the resonance and transference of energies. It is a universal law taught by all the perennial wisdom traditions that *Like attracts Like*. A person is liable to attract the positive just as they can attract the negative. One's interior mental state is thus a valve to exterior energies and conditions. Being mindful of one's thoughts and state of mind is primary to a disciplined management of personal energy.

The 'attention distracter' (AD) that is life increasingly draws a person's attention onto physical events. These events are often of a superficial, vacuous, and inane nature. In this way, ordinary life operates to distract the focused energy of individuals. It is thus necessary for each person to carefully manage their daily mental and emotional energies. For example, we should be wary over putting too much mental attention onto material things. Material objects/events can drain us of our conscious energy, demanding more and more of our awareness. Often, we leak our energy like a bucket with holes.

Technology too can 'gadget-ize' us with our mental energies, making multi-tasking an energy-draining enterprise rather than energy-accumulating. As with everything, we each need to be aware of how much we are being drawn into an event or encounter. It is surprising how quickly our mental energies can be drawn away from us like kids to toys. When we engage ourselves externally we should be aware of the quantity and quality of the energy transaction involved.

If an external influence impacts upon our mental state, as in feeling stressed or confused, then we should create a mental 'stop'. Assess the situation and restart by calling forth and generating *intent*. By putting deliberate mental intention into a situation or event, a person is creating an energetic force that both fuels and protects a person. Rather than being lost at sea, we should direct our paddling towards dry land. Similarly, to alter a disagreeable state of mind a person should seek out those activities that can create a harmonious vibration. For example, when the mind is confused or frustrated, listen to some relaxing music. Or go for a favorite walk in the woods or a place near to Nature. By engaging in activities that create a favorable resonance, a person's energies are revitalized and the 'leak' is plugged. This is a necessary practice when dealing with energy management. After all, if you had a pot of gold you wouldn't go about throwing out handfuls of gold coins. Why do the same with the quantity of personal energy? Therefore, we should always be aware of our mental states since within each moment *everything is Mind*.

A well-known dictum that expresses the situation is *Energy flows where attention goes*. By being aware of where we place our attention, and to what degree, we are better placed to manage our store of energy. The human mind is itself in a state of potential evolution. Hermetic teachings state that:

> Mind (as well as metals and elements) may be transmuted from state to state; degree to degree; condition to condition; pole to pole; vibration to vibration.[27]

A person thus requires enough personal energy if they are to continue with their ongoing evolution. By wasting energy a person is forfeiting the inheritance of their resources for their development.

It is likely that increased energies will be made available during this present epoch. As described earlier, there are cultural interventions which facilitate accelerated social and personal change. It can be said that we are passing through one of these cultural shifts at present. Thus, with more energy 'in the system' it presents an opportunity (and need) for the efficient and creative utilization of these energies. As this short book attempts to explain, some of our energy resources need to be directed towards shifting our cognitive systems and developing our internal-external bridge of communication. This can help each of us to attain our aims toward a future we wish to see for ourselves and for others to come. It is all about being *vigilant with oneself*; a subject to which I now turn.

A TALE TO FINISH:

Be Useless and Enjoy

Lao Tse was traveling with his disciples when they came to a forest where hundreds of loggers were cutting down the trees. The whole forest had been cleared except for a single large tree with hundreds of branches. This one tree was so great that thousands of people could sit within its shade. Lao Tse asked his disciples to go and enquire why it was that this tree had not been cut down. Soon the disciples returned with the answer to their question and told the teacher:

'They say that this tree is completely useless and that nothing can be done with it - its branches are so full of knots and nothing is straight; it is no good for furniture. Also, it cannot even be used for firewood because it produces a smoke that is harmful to the eyes.'

Lao Tse nodded his head and, with a smile, said: 'Be like this tree, completely useless, and then you will grow great and thousands of people will find shade under you. Be the last yet move in the world as if you were not. Do not compete, do not try to prove yourself worthy - it is not necessary. Be useless and enjoy.'

Six

Being Vigilant

Each and every one of us is under self-observation: only that we fail to tell ourselves. Perhaps it is now time to take a more active role in our own watchfulness. If we can learn to be more vigilant with ourselves then we are less under the influence of outside forces.

Each day we are swayed this way and that by exterior forces. Some of these are conditioning forces that exist in social institutions. Other forces, such as propaganda, are deliberately spread through the media and social technologies. In response to the majority of these forces we act as the compliant collective. To all purposes the general behavior that manifests in various social forms is mechanical. And the more mechanical human behavior becomes, the more forces we are under the influence of. By exercising self-vigilance a person can learn to become more aware of their presence – the interior – and its interaction with the exterior environment, its forces and influences.

For a start, how many of us are aware of our breathing? It is significant that the most fundamental physical act of our survival passes largely unnoticed. Yet by the simple act of being aware and attentive to our breathing a force of 'present awareness' can enter a person. This doesn't mean that a person should go about totally fixated upon their breathing; or trying to count each breath obsessively. It is about calmly, during the course of the day, bringing the attention to 'observe' the breathing process. Not only can this act bring some measured calm to a person, but also it works to discipline and 'tighten' personal energy. A person will find, after beginning this exercise, that it will gradually become easier and will require less attention. Soon, it will become natural for the attention to keep an almost constant awareness upon the breathing process. After all, breathing has an important function in that it allows for the exhalation of stale gases and cleans the physical system. Deep breathing, especially, helps to regulate and 'tone' the body as it takes in more oxygen. It can also help a person to relax; yet it should never be overdone or forced, as artificial or 'coerced' breathing can lead to hyperventilation. Rather, it is a matter of allowing the breathing to stabilize itself. The breathing should be in harmony with one's own natural rhythm.

The body benefits from a good, balanced intake of oxygen, which is to be neither labored nor short rasps. And to be aware of one's breathing is not the same as being wary. There should be no tension or anxiety involved. A person should not occupy themselves with such questions as 'Am I breathing correctly?' The most appropriate approach is one of relaxed calm, where gentle awareness of breathing can lay the groundwork to a greater sense of cohesion and communication with the body and self. With this attentiveness in place a person is bringing into focus the present moment. Gradually this practice of breathing-awareness should catalyze and bring into play a person's faculties of vigilance and watchfulness.

Another step in developing vigilance is through awareness of one's own 'steps' that are taken within daily life. What this calls for is observation and attention to those times when either action or inaction is required. And in such situations, to always act towards the positive. There are also situations when *positive inaction* is important. When a person can observe and feel when correct action or inaction is required, then this triggers the right use of energy. In our daily lives it is critical that a person uses their store of energy correctly. This involves correct thinking and/or right action at the right time. It is not about being critical of oneself or observing with the intention of finding fault. Self-vigilance is more about producing a state of watchful harmony. This state can then further attract (and benefit from) the positive.

By being more open to positive impacts and situations a person can be more alert to develop and capitalize upon such beneficial moments and conditions. Such moments can also be developed further, and the energies extended. Yet a person should be careful not to contrive or manufacture artificial conditions that are not in genuine harmony with a person's state or inner priorities.

Being vigilant requires that a person be natural and at ease with themselves. They should become used to observing themselves, and feel quietly confident with the relationship. Within this vigilant state a person can also observe their own thought processes, and to exert greater control and discipline over them – not letting them run around like wild tigers causing internal havoc and distress. So it is about being aware also of coincidences, and how these 'serendipitous moments' can be opportunities or circumstances for action.

This disciplined attentiveness to one's own actions, thoughts, and general participation in everyday life does not concern critical judgment or chastising oneself. One can be gently critical, for sure, yet it is all too easy to become hostile towards oneself: and then the blame-game begins. It is necessary to make sure that a person is comfortable with observing themselves, and that they are at ease with their own 'inner homeland'.

A person's 'inner homeland' represents the internal realm with which an individual develops an intimate communication: it is, after all, the place of their essential self. It should therefore become a place of familiar travel, where a person visits regularly and becomes familiar with the taste of the communication. It should also become the place where a person examines themselves from an objective viewpoint. This act of self-observation is an 'inner muscle' that strengthens each time it is used. A person's own homeland is a journey for reflection; to examine and consider recent motivations, actions and their consequences; and for daily recollection. It should be a welcome place where at the end of the day a person can sit down and recollect how the day's events and experiences passed. Such moments form a kind of self-review; yet in these moments of recollection and analysis a person is also retaining energy rather than letting energy dissipate through scatty and unorganized emotional flourishes and remembrances. It is thus important that any review be as objective and as sympathetic to the self as possible. Again, harshness and/or emotional indulgence is no good for the inland journeys. These trips to internally review events are about getting to know yourself better and better, and to live with yourself in a more harmonious relationship. It is essential in these present times of 'attention distraction' (AD) to maximize on moments of quietness and reflection. Even to take just a few minutes each day within a busy schedule can help to calm, balance, and focus personal energies and mental attention. In our industrialized societies time is speeded-up to the maximum rate of revolutions per minute. This needs to be counterbalanced by taking back and insisting to oneself on five or ten minutes per day of visiting one's homeland. In the end, you can influence your time. For example, if you have ten minutes during the day you can listen to some music; chatter with a friend; batter yourself with mental worries; or enter a state of balanced self-vigilance. While you may not be able to dictate the length of your time, you most certainly can influence the *sense* of your time.

To exercise self-vigilance and to 'travel within' is a learning journey: a path to better know your strengths and weaknesses; and to get to understand what you do and do not know. Yet to accomplish this, a person needs also to exercise a certain degree of balanced humility. There is a joke about this: there were three monks arguing as to which order was the best – the Jesuit, the Benedictine, and the Dominican. After hearing the Jesuit and the Benedictine, the Dominican says: "For logic and argument and organization we all know that the Jesuits are best; and the Benedictines are best for their friendliness and for their great wine; but when it comes to humility, we Dominicans are really the best!" It takes a lot to be genuine and sincere with oneself. Yet by exercising such traits a person is actually strengthening not only their inner discipline but also their command of physical, mental, and emotional energies.

The priority in *breaking the spell* focuses upon the layers of conditioning that a person functions within. A person who is thirty or forty years old has thirty or forty years of conditioning; this cannot be dealt with quite as easily. The question is not about dropping all conditioning like a sack of old clothes – this would literally be a bombshell and may do more harm than good. Also, without some form of social conditioning we would find it very hard to get along in our everyday lives. So conditioning is required *to a degree* in order for us to live communal lives with the people around us (such as conditioning around social politeness). The question, rather, revolves around being made aware of what conditioning is operating at a given time; how it is operating within us; and whether we actually need it or not. And if not, how can we 'halt' or sidestep these conditioned beliefs. According to the Counsels of Bahauddin:

7 – Be prepared to realize that all beliefs which were due to your surroundings were minor ones, even though they were once of much use to you. They may become useless and, indeed, pitfalls.

8 – Be prepared to find that certain beliefs are correct, but that their meaning and interpretation may vary in accordance with your stage of journey, making them seem contra-dictory.[28]

The intention behind vigilance is to stimulate a degree of awareness so that a person may be in a better position to observe their forms of conditioning (physical, mental, and emotional). A person can then develop upon this knowledge to gain a better understanding of themselves. Developing awareness involves a level of discipline that in turn helps to focus an individual's personal energies. The qualities (vibrational nature) of such energies are important in that within a universe of Mind (where everything is energy) all thoughts, words, and deeds carry their own vibratory quality. These energies affect the quality of life of a person, their environment, and the people around them. Therefore, what each person 'puts out', so to speak, is their own responsibility. Within such a conscious universe each of us should learn how to behave. This does not imply being 'more-than-human'; rather, we are asked to be more *fully human*.

There are moments when it is not only possible but desirable to step more lightly, which means not overindulging in situations and/or emotional matters. As is often said, it is not what happens to you that is important but rather how you deal with it. This requires 'strengthening the muscle' of one's disciplined vigilance. For example, with emotional energy it is all too easy to give it away through petty encounters and ignoble disputes. Remember that to feel angry at other people means that you consider their acts/words to have importance – whereas this is often not the case. So why let it drain you? Again quoting the Counsels of Bahauddin:

18 – When you have observed or felt emotion, correct this by remembering that emotions are felt just as strongly by people with completely different beliefs. If you imagine that this experience – emotion – is therefore noble or sublime, why do you not believe that stomach ache is an elevated state?[29]

People can waste an incredible amount of time feeling offended by the words and/or deeds of others. To feel offended is a form of self-indulgence that succeeds in making the inner person lazy. If you feel offended, you worry too much about others and care less about yourself.

54

Physical energy too also requires a healthy and balanced management. We can learn to be attentive to our physical positions: when seated, standing, or in movement. We can watch how we move and note which movements are most comfortable for us. And also how we sit – which positions are more favorable and conducive to a sense of well-being and comfort. We should aim to become more conscious of our physical movements and more aware of our body positions. A person should aim to be conscious when eating, for example, and to be aware of the senses: smell, taste, touch, sight and hearing. The intention here is not to become automatic to the senses. This form of self-vigilance involves a sensing of the being and the body. Within this awareness a person takes some time to sense how the body is generally feeling, to see if there is any unconscious stress or imbalance within the system. And if there is an imbalance you should know that you have the competence to deal with it.

So in this state a person is sensing their inner self and assessing its condition. Further, each individual should be able to distinguish between a 'normal' pain, such as a headache, for instance, and a sort of nagging inside which is the inner self trying to communicate.

This communication bridge to the inner self should be strengthened – to polish the bridge within.

Also, a person can help to direct energy to specific areas of the body by focusing their attention: '*Energy flows where attention goes*'. We can make conscious use of our energy to be mentally alert and energetically attentive during physical processes. And this includes also the realm of human sexuality.

Sexual energy is one of the strongest forces operating within and between humans. It can be very animalistic when energetic power is enforced upon the 'pacified other'. Or it can be more fully human when there is a harmonious union with individual integrity; a sharing yet retaining of energies. Sexuality should not become a form of mutual dependency where both partners have a need to absorb rather than to share energy (a form of mutual vampirism). If both consenting partners are aware of the energies involved in the sexual exchange, this awareness can enhance the physical union. So even during these intimate moments the act of vigilance (watchfulness) can play an important role. Also, such positive moments should be memorized and then recalled when needed. The deliberate recollection of stored positive moments can help to stimulate positive energy. Thus, at times of low energy this technique of positive recollection can help to release affirming energies within a person.

Being vigilant also involves being on the alert for people, places, moments and experiences that have a positive energy. That is, being open to impacts of a positive nature. One should be open and 'scanning' for harmonic encounters – as positive contacts may come in forms not expected and be unpredictable. An individual should be open to all possibilities.

Unpredictable encounters and impacts are available even within the everyday life of most people. This does not mean that one cannot earn a reasonable living, and be exposed to the blows and distractions that being in the world delivers, and still be able to open oneself. The balance concerns being both 'in the world' while maintaining a healthy and harmonious inner self and integrity 'not of the world'. A person can be exposed and subjected to external stresses and still remain master of their internal self. There does not need to be a conflict, or a 'sacrifice'. The inner self of an individual needs to be defended and simultaneously enhanced and strengthened. If a person gives in and conforms to all of their social conditioning, then they use up valuable energy that could have been used for inner work. For this reason, it is important to be aware when social conditioning is operating; and to observe its working. In this manner part of the social 'spell' can be broken. Another important aspect of *breaking the spell* is knowing when negativity is acting within and against a person.

Let it be said that the main function of the negative is to disturb and disrupt a person's energy flows. Negativity seeks to distract a person's thinking and shift it away from the positive. Negativity by itself has no capacity for control; it seeks only to exploit vulnerable situations and circumstances. For example, if a person's state is not fully balanced the negative will try to 'sneak in' to give a further push away from the positive. In this case a person needs to exercise discipline and be on the lookout for negative intrusions. When negativity is sensed within a person they need to act quickly as it often takes longer for the positive to 'wake up' and counteract the situation. In normal circumstances, however, the average person has between 10–15% negativity within them (and often less). Yet when the positive is less alert than the negative, a person can be momentarily taken over by negative impulses if they are not careful. The positive needs more time to kick in and get the situation under control. This is why *being vigilant* is so important when guarding the self against unwanted impacts, intrusions, and loss of personal energy.

And society does not help the matter. Generally, social contexts and circumstances concur to magnify certain negative impulses and traits. If a person's social environment is more exposed to negative impacts (from work or people) the more imperative it is to be on guard during these situations. The negative is nothing to be feared; otherwise there is the tendency to give it more importance than it deserves. Try to remember that every negative experience contains its own learning factor. In general, negativity seeks confusion; to react against the opposing energy which is balance and harmony. Negative energy thus acts to disturb harmonious and developmental thinking. Yet it cannot control you or take you over – unless you yourself give power to the negative energy. It is also a matter of how a person *perceives* the matter at hand. All of us, at some point, have been faced with a problem; yet for most of the time we are faced with daily situations. Every problem is also a situation, yet not every situation is a problem. First ask yourself what you have: is it a *problem* or a *situation*? Once a person knows this they are better equipped to deal with the matter, and with an appropriate investment of energies.

If there is a feeling/sense of disharmony with certain events or circumstances, then one should try to define the reason for this lack of harmony. Once identified, a person can then introduce positive thoughts and intentions into the situation. For example, before entering a situation that you know will make you tense, nervous, or angry (such as a relationship or job interview), prepare beforehand by creating a positive charge of energy within yourself. *Being vigilant* with oneself is also about being prepared – and energetically armed!

Again – *The communication bridge to the inner self should be strengthened - to polish the bridge within.*

Listen to this communication and be vigilant for warning signals: are you attracting the negative? An individual, a group, even a nation can receive warning signals of the negative. No one goes to ruin 'innocently'!

When a person is being vigilant of their internal and external worlds a greater amount of energy is made available. This energy is useful in attracting the positive and in dealing with everyday impacts. In this state a person can perform to the best of their ability and capacity. And due to the law of 'reciprocal influence', all actions create an influence in the world that will manifest in some way. Therefore, one should think and behave impeccably. How we measure ourselves also mirrors how we measure the world around us: we share the same terms of reference. If we are at fault, so do we also perceive our world to be at fault. If we are vigilant with ourselves we will refrain from jumping to conclusions or making assumptions. We will be more aware of our external influences; where they come from; how they impact against the self; and how we ultimately respond. This is a genuine bridge of communication between the external world of social conditioning, and our internal world of the intuitive and deep self. And once this bridge of communication is formed it will always remain. However lightly or mildly the contact is used it can never be lost. Like a muscle it needs to be strengthened and developed through use.

Being vigilant is one technique for dealing with the everyday social world of distracting influences and impacts. The other technique is what is named as *stepping away.*

A TALE TO FINISH:

The Lion

A lion was captured and imprisoned in a reserve where, to his surprise, he found other lions that had been there for many years, some even their whole life having been born in captivity. The newcomer soon became familiar with the activities of the other lions, and observed how they were arranged in different groups.

One group was dedicated to socializing, another to show business, whilst yet another group was focused on preserving the customs, culture and history from the time the lions were free. There were church groups and others that had attracted the literary or artistic talent. There were also revolutionaries who devoted themselves to plot against their captors and against other revolutionary groups. Occasionally, a riot broke out and one group was removed or killed all the camp guards and so that they had to be replaced by another set of guards. However, the newcomer also noticed the presence of a lion that always seemed to be asleep. He did not belong to any group and was oblivious to them all. This lion appeared to arouse both admiration and hostility from the others. One day the newcomer approached this solitary lion and asked him which group he belonged to.

'Do not join any group' said the lion, 'those poor ones deal with everything but the essentials.'

'And what is essential?' asked the newcomer.

'It is essential to study the nature of the fence'

Seven

Stepping Away

The technique of *stepping away* involves a person being able to detach from situations that they may find distracting, noisy, or confusing. What this suggests is that a person should be able to move inward for a short time when they feel it necessary to have some space away from tensions, or events that are antagonistic or disruptive to one's state. It is also about *stepping away* from using all of one's physical faculties in order to conserve energy. For example, if you are sitting quietly you don't need all your senses on full awareness. Sometimes it can be beneficial to drop oneself into a lower running gear, as if ticking-over. A person should learn when to not only step back from physical engagements, but also from emotional attachments and other involvements of the senses. This can be achieved through various moments throughout the day: five minutes here or there. It can be done on the underground/subway, in the car or on a bus. You don't need to detach to the point that you are not aware of external circumstances – this can be particularly dangerous if you are in the car or on the street! It is about shifting your priorities of internal and external involvement.

A person can successfully insulate themselves from unnecessary external noises and impacts by a reasonable and calm organized withdrawal. There is no need to put cotton wool in the ears. This technique can be used whenever it is felt to be appropriate – there is no hard and fast rule. As in everything, it depends upon a person's circumstances and their state of being. It also allows for a person to create moments throughout the day for quiet reflection; moments to halt the flow of chatter. These can be small moments to be enjoyed, and that refreshes one mentally and physically. In a sense, it is like taking a break; only that the break is often in the middle of everyday life. For example, you are travelling on the underground (subway/metro), and the carriage is packed full of commuters all squeezed together with an armada of free newspapers. There is the screech of brakes, the hum of the train, the almost inaudible buzz of music seeping through earphones. The situation is both disturbing and stressful. Why should you always begin your day like this? So: *step back within yourself.* Pull your focus inward, turn down some of your senses, recollect some fond memories, or recite some words to yourself. Don't allow the external impacts to affect you, or to enter into your inner space.

There is no need to leave the world behind: you still need to be relatively alert in case there is a madman loose in the carriage. You only need to *step away* from the bustle of external impacts and impressions. In effect you are suspending a part of your social involvement. You are conserving your 'self' and your energies. Involved in this is also a measured degree of restraint. Exercising restraint means imposing self-discipline in that you are avoiding conditioned reactions and sudden impulses. As in *being vigilant* a person can, after observation, decide to refrain from exercising conditioned responses. Such impulses, judgments, preconceived attitudes are put to one side. This is a halting, or *stepping away*, from indulging in particular social terms of reference. A person is thus learning to restrain themselves at specific moments when conditioned factors and references come into play. Yet this technique also suggests that at times a physical withdrawal is necessary.

Being able to *step away* requires a person to exercise patience. It also means that sometimes inaction is as valuable as action (depending on the circumstance, of course!). So patience can be used to assess the situation. Some situations may demand instantaneous action, whereas others may be better served by the person restraining from involvement. Of course, there needs to be a modicum of common sense. If there is a car hurtling towards you, you get yourself out of the way as quickly as possible. This is no time for exercising patience with the car driver by letting yourself get hit and squashed. No one will say – "What a shame, yet they did manifest the most admirable patience with that car driver." They will most likely say – "What an idiot!"

So *stepping away* infers exercising patience and restraint **under the right conditions** until a situation is better understood. The alternative may be an impulsive response based on layers of conditioning. So if you are not sure about how to act within a particular situation, pull back a little and show some personal restraint. By doing this you are in fact looking after yourself. You are learning how to detach from unnecessary baggage, whether mental or emotional. This also helps a person to refrain from acts of pettiness and unwarranted attachment. Forms of pettiness and attachment are traits that quickly drain personal energies, and in the end become something that a person is unable to let go of. There is an old dervish story about this:

There were two dervishes travelling together. One of them was old and the other was the younger student. They had travelled together for many years; all the time the younger student believing he was learning to be righteous in the shadow of his teacher. His own belief in value of his actions gave him faith along his Path. One day both travellers came to a river crossing. Yet the water had recently risen and was waist high. At the side of the river was a young attractive lady, sensual yet distressed. She was afraid of water and sought help in crossing.

The younger student immediately shunned her as he felt it was not right for him to touch such a lady who was clearly disreputable. Suddenly, without hesitation, the older dervish picked up the young lady, slung her on his back, and carried the young woman across the river. When he got to the other side he put her down and carried on walking. Not a word was spoken.

The young dervish hurried after his teacher, surprised and bewildered. He could not believe that his teacher, whom he had trusted and followed all these years, could act in such an immodest way. The young man was fuming. He wanted to confront the older man yet knew it best to keep quiet until a suitable moment. All day though the younger student trailed behind the older man, shaking his head and cursing himself for wasting so many years. The whole day went on like this. The younger man's faith was in turmoil. Finally, they came to a place where the older dervish wanted to rest for the night. They sat in silence for a while.

Knowingly, the older dervish finally smiled and said to the younger one: "Now you can tell me what is on your mind."

The younger man spilled his day's frustrations and anger; his incredulity at the other's 'non-spiritual' behavior. When he had finished ranting the older dervish quietly turned to the young man and said:

"I picked that woman up and carried her across the river. When I got to the other side I put her down. **But you are still carrying her.**"[30]

That which we cannot refrain from becomes our extra baggage. We are, as in the ancient edict, our own worst enemies. We often get pulled into situations by our own desire for attention and self-esteem. Yet by 'inflating' our self for others we diminish our own being. We need to be aware of when to give attention and when to step away and refrain from giving attention. People rarely understand the fact that each one of us craves attention. It is like food for us; from our childhood, to adulthood, and even to the end of our days. So *stepping away* is another technique for working with one's attention: when to be active and when to be inactive. This swing between the two poles of activity and inactivity also marks out the strong presence of polarity within human lives.

Everyday life in the human world can be likened to a polarity game; a pendulum swing between opposites. We only know what is 'hot' because we understand what is 'cold'; we understand there is 'darkness' because we have the experience of 'light'. Things in the physical world are known by their opposition: forces that are active and passive exert themselves upon human lives. Everything and everybody manifests its own polarity. Spirit and matter are extreme degrees of the same essence. Hermetic teachings state that:

> Everything is dual; everything has poles; everything has its pair of opposites; like and unlike are the same; opposites are identical in nature, but different in degree; extremes meet; all truths are but half-truths; all paradoxes may be reconciled.[31]

Polarities trick us into the illusion of taking sides, such as choosing which is the 'winning' side and which the 'losing'. Yet to emotionally feel victorious, or defeated, is an energetic state of our choosing; and one that will demand much from a person. A person pays for taking emotional sides. People spend considerable energies dividing the world into people who are good or evil, rich or poor, intelligent or stupid, important or insignificant. Often standards of 'good' and 'evil' depend upon individual or group criteria, usually handed down through social processes, and are not objective fact.

And all too often people spend much of their lives categorizing what they 'like' and what they 'dislike'. A person 'likes' these clothes, this style, at this time; then 'dislikes' them at a later time. A person 'likes' this person at this time, then 'dislikes' them a moment later. This is an easy trap to fall into, a continuing cycle of likes/dislikes that force a person to make mental and emotional attachments that distract the attention and drain personal energies. Within such polarities a person is forced to make judgments. Sometimes it is better if a person refrains from judging. It is harder to find contentment and happiness within a world of continual judgments. Remember the words of the New Testament: "Why do you look at the speck of sawdust in your brother's eye and pay no attention to the plank in your own eye?" (Matthew 7:3). Too much external distraction takes the attention away from the real source within a person. And there are forces too in the physical world that deliberately create strongly polarized energies (fear, stress, tension) in order to disrupt the formation of balanced polarities.

So we should refrain from too easily jumping into the polarity game: *step away* and view the processes more objectively. In truth, it is not about our likes or dislikes. This is an emotional seesaw that sways a person from one encounter to the next. A person who moves between likes and dislikes will find it more difficult to achieve harmony in their life. Hakim Sanai, an 11th century Persian poet, wrote that:

'Good' and 'evil' have no meaning in the world of the Word: they are names, coined in the world of 'me' and 'you'.[32]

Getting tied into polarities, between 'beliefs and 'non-beliefs', is itself a subjective entanglement supplied by the physical world. After all, belief in 'non-belief' is still a belief.

Polarity then is a way of fixing one's attention onto externalities: we are generous or mean; we indulge or deny; we do 'good' or 'bad'. However, it is often the case that by following attachment to a particular polarity a person is in fact indulging more. For example, the urge in some people to do 'good' (the 'do-gooders') is often a need to feel self-gratification, which is an internal reward. It is a form of greed. Yet greed to be generous is still greed; to indulge in our denial is still indulgence. Often, the 'desire' to be *this* or *that* is in fact a need to indulge our desires. There is no simple and pure act as long as a person exists through polarity. It is an illusion we rarely see and thus it draws a person in almost completely.

Polarity makes a person see events and challenges as a blessing or a curse. We rarely see them as simply events; moreover, events that we are asked to respond to. Being influenced by the swing of the pendulum that is polarity can create challenges and stress. It can be a struggle to try to find 'one's place' within the contradictory nature of active and passive forces. By *stepping away* a person can practice a form of patience that allows them to have a more objective understanding of events and influences. We may not be able to escape the effects of polarity completely, yet we can shift ourselves to a more harmonious position. Physical life will ensure that the pendulum will continue to swing; only that with awareness and restraint we may escape being carried along with it:

> Perhaps it is only by standing back, emotionally, and testing our assumptions that we can become more the masters of ourselves and correspondingly less the slaves of circumstance.[33]

Responsibility to oneself involves taking the opportunities to act properly, whether this means through action or inaction. A degree of restraint – and patience – can enable this capacity to function more effectively. To *step away* thus involves an awareness of physical and emotional participation within circumstances, events, experiences, and beliefs.

Stepping away also involves an inward move (or 'shift') for a short time when a person feels it necessary to detach from noisy or distracting situations. It is about being aware of how to conserve one's personal energies. In a modern world that, for most, is an amplified 'Attention Distracter' (AD), this is a useful and functional technique. After all, as we walk our individual paths we need to preserve the clarity of our perceptions.

A TALE TO FINISH:

Two Men

Two men who were unjustly imprisoned for a long time shared a cell together where they received all sorts of abuse and humiliation at the hands of the prison guards. Finally they were both freed and, after many years, ran into each other one day in the street. One of them asked the other:

'Do you ever remember the guards and how they treated us?'

'No, thank God, I've forgotten everything', said the other. 'What about you?'

'I've continued hating them with all my strength' he replied. His friend looked at him a moment, then said:

'I feel for you. If so, it means you are still imprisoned.'

Eight

Perception – It's a Matter of Perspective

The development of human perception is still often regarded as 'spooky', or as not a 'normal' pursuit, whereas in truth it is very necessary. It is accurate to say that a person has potential beyond their dreams. So much so that dreams sometimes inhibit a person because they cannot perceive deep enough or far enough.

Higher perception is a faculty that when operative is able to distinguish between what is information – the assembly of facts – and what is knowledge. While not everyone has the faculty of higher perception operating within them, many have the capacity to acquire it. There have always been a number of individuals within humanity that have aspired toward acquiring a higher functioning degree of perception. The efforts to achieve this have always been varied and with mixed results. It is therefore important that society, with its numerous forms of conditioning, does not dilute or distract these aims into lesser objectives. The focus and intention must remain resolute and committed. Many 'metaphysical ways' are discarded forms of previous teachings aimed at raising human consciousness (like a caterpillar that sheds its chrysalis). A person must ensure that they do not become distracted by attraction to a non-functional and deteriorated system. Perception within a person is that which is able to recognize between information and knowledge; and between secondary (decayed) and primary (genuine) traces of real inner wisdom and insight.

Many so-called 'spiritual teachings' have fallen to a lower level than their original functioning. Many now operate through repetition and/or emotional release mechanisms. In such systems there is an absence of real experience; replaced instead by subjective experience that the person takes to be significant, and an indicator of 'higher knowledge'. This relates to what was said previously: that 'False gold only exists because there is such thing as the Real'. It is like arriving in a new country for the first time and finding that all the citizens wear different parts of a computer as fashion accessories – they are trendy; they look good; they are the 'next best thing'; they imply status, etc – yet no one knows that the parts should be put together, or how, in order to produce a functioning whole: a computer. So too is much spiritual knowledge in this day and age so scattered, misunderstood, and inappropriately used. It is a characteristic of our human conditioning to collect various fragments and to consider this gathering together as a profitable and worthwhile enterprise – like going to a flea market and coming back with a handful of bargains. In the same way, people often feel that by collecting, dabbling, in various metaphysical-spiritual subjects – gathering bits of 'useful' information – that they are learning and developing upon a correct inner path. Yet the haphazard collection of shiny objects will not necessarily produce a functioning system. And it is highly doubtful that it ever will. This is a matter of perception, which needs to be developed upon. For this reason a degree of personal perception is crucial in recognizing the wheat from the chaff.

Perception can be like trying to explain color to a blind person. Our over-reliance upon a stagnant form of intellectualism obstructs the true growth of our finer perceptions. Once the bars of intellectual imprisonment have been removed there is the possibility for more subtle modes of perception to operate. The previous sentence **must not** be grasped as an intellectual hypothesis. Our conditioning (intellectual, emotional, mental) often creates a fight with those impacts and influences that could be most beneficial to us – just as a drowning person may fight off their rescuers amid the struggle. What we can do to help the 'rescue' is to shift our perspectives and their emphasis of attention: away from forms of dogma (linearity, regulations, ritual, etc) onto more conceptual forms that can be learned through experience. In other words, lose the linearity and make friends with the conceptual!

Too many people, too much of the time, wish to talk about the various 'shiny pieces' and not about the whole; and often attempt to persuade others to exalt and praise the virtue of the pieces as if to validate their worth. With correct perspective, a person can 'step away' from these fruitless enterprises and focus upon the inner whole. Remember: having more cannot compensate us for being less.

Our finer perceptions may at first seem like a stranger to us; yet this is only through disuse, like an underused or slack muscle. Perception requires exercise; it is a matter of correct perspective. To enable correct perspective a person needs to practice discernment, and an awareness of presence and energy – as discussed in the previous chapters. The right kind of perspective, under the right conditions, can develop a person – and help to *break the spell*. One step to begin this is to familiarize oneself with these ideas, to grasp them and feel their worth; yet not intellectually nor emotionally but with an inner organ of discernment. As the saying goes, the bird with its beak in salt water all year round does not know fresh water.

If a person is not ready – not 'equipped' – to perceive certain things then these things do not exist for the person. Perceptions that are suited to present conditions may be lower than those perceptions that may be possible for a person to achieve. It is important to recognize (to *perceive*) that levels of development are always possible and that the 'present moment' only represents a stage along the way, and is almost never final. If you do not, or cannot, understand something then you can do little about it.

Each of us, in varying degrees, has the perception that we need to move forward. Some perceive it as an urge; others as a desire; or as a niggling suspicion. By not correctly acting, with perception, on this impulse humankind is open to a sense of dissatisfaction, which can increase according to the influence of external circumstances. In short, humanity has the function to move forward along its evolutionary destiny. The danger is that elements within our human societies may create false substitutes that provide temporary 'fulfillment'. If our perceptions are limited to a lower capacity, then they are vulnerable to attracting stimuli, impulses, influences, etc that feed these perceptions and which perpetuate the entrapment of our perception. These are our 'narcotic distractions' that come in many forms and which serve to distract us – to put a 'spell' on us – and thus artificially yet deliberately interfere with our capacity and potentials.

In such states of diminished perception it becomes easy for the human mind to change its thinking and to start to believe that all current circumstances are a result of 'fate'. Therefore, such experiences/states as uncertainty, insecurity, incompleteness, etc are all part of 'fate's struggle' and are forces that a person must accept in their lives. The extreme of this thinking is to view emptiness as a valid state in life: this perspective is nihilistic, or at best pseudo-existentialist. The forces of inertia must be overcome. To lose the force of forward momentum in our lives is to surrender to the 'spell' of our life's conditioning. Internal energy must be provided in order to overcome the obstacles of external inertia. In other words, each person is required to make an individual effort to develop their perception, and thus increase their energetic state. Through self-development of perception a person can break free from distorted realities, from erratic energetic environments, and to glimpse other 'realities'. We have the capacity to define the fabric of our own perceptions, and to seek corresponding stimuli. It is our responsibility to extend our own tools of perception. There is no better time than the present to begin breaking our old perceptual patterns because humanity now has assistance: it is *timely*. That is, the evolutionary impulse that is now making its presence felt within humanity and upon the Earth facilitates changing patterns. It will be easier to break away from ingrained patterns – mentally, emotionally, and behaviorally – than at any other time in our present existence. In such periods, it is possible to make radical re-patterning and to develop perceptual insights.

Perception is a form of deep intuition, which means learning to trust our insights. We can begin by familiarizing ourselves with the *taste* of our intuitions; to follow them, a little at first until we gain confirmation of their correctness. As we receive validation of our intuitions both the signals forthcoming and our recognition and action on them will increase. This will confirm to us the truth of our own inner perceptions, until such taste becomes almost second nature to us.

We don't need to have expectations of immediately perceiving and understanding the bigger picture – the so-called 'Grand Design' – but we can begin by working to see how the smaller picture begins with oneself. A good way to start is by setting small yet achievable goals that can be accomplished. As previously described, we should begin by focusing and training our intentions, and to support these intentions with the appropriate energy. Working step-by-step, in incremental phases, we can develop ourselves to a more fully responsible human being in the world. This is a true goal of spiritual work on oneself: to be *fully human.*

What is important in these times is to gain L.I.F.E. – to Live an Integrated Fulfilling Existence. Yet as many ancient mystics and spiritual teachers have stated – people will do almost anything to avoid working on themselves! To aim for L.I.F.E we will need balanced emotions of positivity, creativity, motivation, and enthusiasm. Also, we will need to be perceptive of our emotional states and to avoid being sucked down into the negative emotional trappings of fear, helplessness, and insecurity. There is the danger that we get caught-up in a world of increasing acceleration and we give diminishing time and attention to the 'timeless' resources within us. We become too distracted to the time-orientated life outside of us; in contrast, our timeless realm inside seems to us to have no power, no attraction, no control (or no 'place') in our outer existence. We may allow ourselves a brief ten minutes of meditation in our busy lives to connect with our inner 'timeless space'; and then we shelve it, relegate it to an ephemeral side of us that we only speak to in rare moments or when stressed. We fail to see that it is exactly this part of us which has the capacity to enhance each physical moment, to infuse the external with our energy signatures.

It is beneficial to be perceptive of when the emotional level is too engaged as this leaves little or no energy left over for spiritual activity. It is important to realize that there is a difference between learning something and feeling good. The priority is to be balanced, and to have harmony and equilibrium: happiness comes naturally from these states. One of the secrets is to restrict emotionality to areas where it can be useful and functional. We know that if we overeat we get obese; yet there is no similar measure about the intake of emotion. Much of our 'cultural nutrition', especially in the West, is charged with emotion – call it high-calorie emotion. This causes confusion, reinforces habits of conditioning, and is an obstacle in the way of refining perception and self-observation. We need to begin to measure our emotional intake, be able to dose it, and to stop binging on it.

Capacities within each of us can be stimulated and exercised, just like a muscle, and which operate more clearly when a person is free from obsessional tendencies, heedlessness, over-anxiety, and over-dramatization. Thus, balance and equilibrium is the real issue to be solved. Normal human behavior is to seek emotional satisfaction out of every situation, whether good or bad. Many religious groupings use service, either consciously or unconsciously, as a means for people to discharge ambition and/or ego. There is an old oral tale that tells of a rich merchant who, nearing the end of his life, wanted to give something back to the community after all of his devious trading in past years. So he paid a vast amount of wealth for the construction of a magnificent church that stood in the center of his town. When the beautiful edifice was completed the merchant ordered a golden plaque to be placed over the front entrance with the words: 'This house of prayer has been generously provided by...' and the merchant's name was put proudly for all to see. A few years later the merchant died and on arriving at the pearly gates of heaven he met with St. Peter who looked into the illustrious register of people's lives to see if they are worthy to enter the Kingdom of Heaven. St. Peter went through each of the merchant's misdemeanors one by one until there was a conspicuous list. After this he then went through the merchant's positive contributions until, finally, the merchant found himself down by one positive contribution. "But," stammered the merchant, "I built that beautiful church near the end of my life. Surely this is enough to compensate and to get me into heaven?" St. Peter shook his head slowly and replied – "I'm afraid you received your reward for that one while you were still on Earth."

I guess you can't get rewarded twice!

Many of us continue to be caught-up in our traditions, histories, rituals, and formalities – not realizing it is these very same things that serve to block us from perceiving the subtlety of our current reality. It is as if we are a train on its track, restrained in its direction by the fixed route of the rails, and not able to veer off onto other paths. We are almost completely unaware of how our cultures are full of suggestions, offering avenues of opportunities in one direction but not another. We therefore need to be on guard against and be aware of such suggestions, particularly critical/negative ones. We can be completely fenced in, immobilized, by suggestions that disempower us; that persuade us to conform, that tell us something isn't possible or should not be tried. We would do well to remember that such negative or disempowering criticisms more often than not come from those who are unable to validate that which is outside the remit of their perceptions. How can such criticisms be valid when most of the time their judgment of familiar things is faulty?

To summarize, people tend to behave within either of two camps: i) within the normal conditioned mode, as produced by their localized culture and environment; or ii) in reaction against the cultural norms. Yet both these display a polarized way of being. There is another, more productive and beneficial way: manifesting a certain form of perception – consciousness – which gives one a different perspective on circumstances and events. It is possible to cultivate this subtle form of perception because it is working within each of us all the time; we are only not aware of it because of our reliance upon the other two modes. It is important to increase one's perception of it, which can be achieved by the previous 'steps', such as self-vigilance, stepping away, and increased awareness of our energy states. Such perception – or deep intuition – within a person cannot be verified by ordinary means. Rather, it carries its own form of self-validation; that is, by a person 'obtaining' information that cannot be acquired by any other way. This means of working toward *breaking the spell* is not for any moral or ethical purpose – in the sense of human moral systems – but because it clears the way for a heightened form of perception to operate. Such procedures and 'steps' toward *breaking the spell* should be approached quietly, calmly, and gently – not with typical human fanfare.

However, we need to allow things to disturb our attitudes and assumptions, to stimulate us to think about things which are different from our familiar patterns. This then provides us with a certain flexibility. There is no other way to capture or understand a sense of 'meaning' in our lives other than to become conscious to it. We must therefore work on developing our consciousness. Perhaps the first step is to begin changing our minds.

A TALE TO FINISH:

A Change of Mind

God decided to come down to Earth for a quick look at how his creation was coming along.

He approached Earth and happened to look at a big tree full of howling monkeys. As He looked down, one of the monkeys happened to look up and saw him.

The monkey became excited and started to shout:
'I see God.....I see God!'

None of the other monkeys paid any attention. Some thought the monkey was crazy or perhaps just a religious fanatic. They went on about their daily lives of collecting food, taking care of their young, fighting with each other, etc., etc. Not getting any attention, our monkey decided to try to get attention from God, and said:

'God, Almighty, You are the Beneficent, the Merciful, please help me!'

In an instant, the monkey was transformed into a man living in his own human community. Everything changed, except for one thing: the monkey's mind. The monkey immediately realized that could be a problem.

'Well, thank you God, but what about my mind?'

'That', said God, 'you will have to change yourself.'

Nine

A Note to Oneself

This final chapter is a note to the 'oneself' of each of us; a reminder of who we are. We have the power of change within ourselves. We only have to think, perceive, and realize that this is true for it to become our truth. Again, we live within a universe that is MINDFUL – where consciousness is primary in a *mind-before-matter* universe. Thus, the future is where you are sitting right now.

In the beginning of this book I talked about how our ancient human ancestors nurtured a greater connection with the living universe. How they internalized affinities and correspondences in order to forge a harmonious relationship with the external physical world. The world of matter was largely conceived of through the sphere of the Mind. Yet today the world of the human being is largely lacking this inherent partnership. Still, there is every reason for the light to shine. As an extract from Jalal ad-Din Rumi's[iii] unpublished diary shows: "I came home dead tired and couldn't even lift my head up, and I asked myself, 'What is the point of all this?' I work like a donkey, and at night I am just tired, what is the point?" And after that he wrote: "The sun rises in the morning."[34]

In our world we are blessed by a sun that always rises. And although we live in a universe that is energetic and conscious our terrestrial domain is a world that is very real and physical for us. It is this combination of 'mind' acting upon and through 'matter' that we can create a relationship between our external selves and the inner being of our internal world. This is the great alchemical work, the true art of transformation: to "transmute that which is undesirable into that which is worthy, and thus triumph."[35]

The art also is for each individual to live consciously; and not to be an unconscious instrument within the polar forces of human history. We must sense that the universe will provide for and favor those who are in harmony with it. Yet when you have that 'lock-on' it needs to be worked at and developed – not just left to dangle. The relationship of harmonious attraction needs to be maintained.

The human being possesses the necessary equipment for the journey ahead; for the next stage upon our evolutionary path. Jalal ad-Din Rumi also stated that:

New organs of perception come into being as a result of necessity.

Therefore, O man, increase your necessity, so that you may increase your perception.

The human tools – our dormant functions – lie within, awaiting the necessity to awaken. It is our responsibility to create that necessity. It is also our right and endowment to ask for the necessary energy for support.

In the end we are never alone: we are as near or as far from the *center* as we wish ourselves to be. Any sense of separation is what we make it to be. We can say that each person is tied by invisible threads to everyone – and everything – else. Each entity is constantly in a state of invisible reciprocity. Everything we do, big or small, has a bearing and influence upon our future. We do not exist in a vacuum: we are in a sea of vibrant life. So a person acting in ways that are beneficial to themselves is not necessarily engaging in a self-centered activity. Any individual who acts with focused and sincere intention will positively affect those people and circumstances around them. When a person's thought processes are developed and enhanced, this naturally has an influence upon their environment. Each person is involved in an ongoing transmutation process:

The change is not in the nature of a transmutation of one thing into another thing entirely different – but is merely a change of degree in the same things, a vastly important difference.[36]

Transmutation, however, can operate in both directions. Within our often contradictory and ambiguous physical environment it is hoped that consciousness (and conscious humanity) strives for continuing enhancement rather than devolution.

Nothing is ever the way it appears to be. In our physical world those elements that seem opposed are often working together. This is the nature of a 'secondary' world: a shadow from Plato's cave, a reflection of light from its source, a leaf blowing in the wind. Within the physical we 'see' and experience secondary causes. As such, our human 'rationality' is built upon these diluted observations. Yet we do not need to get caught-up within them. Such rationality and 'cleverness' may make a ripple on the surface of the sea, yet they leave no lasting trace. It is helpful to remember that many of our conditioning 'tools' are faulty. Again, as Hakim Sanai wrote:

If you yourself
are upside down in reality,
then your wisdom and faith
are bound to be topsy-turvy.[37]

Sometimes we need to leave such things behind us. There is an old Eastern maxim that reminds a person to leave their donkey at the door and not to ride it into the house. Our social conditionings are useful in that they function to get us to our own front door: then it is best to tie the donkey outside.

There is also the Eastern tale about the wise-fool Nasrudin who was well-known as a smuggler and used to ride his donkey, with his sacks, across the border time and time again. The border guards, knowing of Nasrudin's reputation, used to search his sacks thoroughly each time looking for smuggled items. Yet they never found any, which always puzzled them greatly as they could see that Nasrudin's personal wealth was visibly increasing over time. Eventually, years later when Nasrudin had retired and gone to live in another country, one of the border guards met him. "You can tell me now, Nasrudin, whatever it was you were smuggling that we could never find." "Donkeys," was Nasrudin's reply. Assumptions, such as had the border guards, prevented them from *seeing* what was directly in front of their eyes. The fixed perception limits the field of vision. So too are many of us enmeshed within our own invisible nets of assumptions.

Once we have 'left the donkey outside' (stepped away from our conditionings and assumptions) we can allow the 'unbelievable' and welcome the unpredictable. There is no place for assembly-line thinking (the 'Fordism of thought') within the inner rooms. Outside the house lie many contradictory events that appear to be an affront to various beliefs, ideals, and reasoning. These exist within the swing of the polarity pendulum; they are the trinkets that distract the eye. This is the place where we all worship little things, collected like souvenirs of some visit. They often become the ornaments of a life lived. We decorate ourselves with these symbols. Yet they don't need to be brought into the house. We can leave them outside – they are going nowhere.

Within the internal self there are no contradictions. There just *is*. The creative, intuitive self lies within the Heart of humankind. So where do we go from here?

The human species is on a remarkable journey of evolutionary enhancement. It is a path of consciousness as true human evolution is the evolution of conscious perception. It is an energetic journey filled with forces that bind all of us – individually and collectively – to a larger cosmos. Within this cosmic environment specific evolutionary laws operate. And such laws have been in operation all throughout Earth history. These are the deeper laws that penetrate all appearances. As spoken of earlier, these are the creative forces that have operated behind the rise and fall of consecutive societies and civilizations. Each successive wave, each renewal, is part of the ongoing process of human, cultural, and spiritual evolution. If we can understand this we are better prepared to shift into new and enlightening cognitive systems. And it is paramount that we now assist ourselves, our loved ones, and those of our immediate environments, in this accelerated stage of transformation. Each genuine act of energetic sincerity *does produce a positive effect*. Nothing gets wasted.

Recent upheavals in our physical world are reactions to intensifying evolutionary energies. Physically and spiritually we are converging towards a necessary future. There is nothing to be feared. It is time to deactivate the old programming, the old anxieties and tensions. We are now called upon to prepare the human *being* for a rapid period of development and change. It is time to *Break the Spell*; a time to activate and enhance our own energetic change. Each one of us has the necessary tools and the inherent capacity. We only require the intention and the commitment.

The bigger picture is slowly breaking into view. And we are all travelling towards an immense event with an accelerating speed. The next stage in the evolutionary journey of humanity will be astounding. What matters most during these times is our state of consciousness.

The future is here – if you can take it...

A TALE TO FINISH:

Light

Song Hu, an Eastern philosopher, told his disciples the following story:

Several men had been imprisoned by mistake in a dark cave where they could see almost nothing. Time passed and one of them managed to light a small torch. But the light it gave was so scarce that even with it hardly anything could be seen. It occurred to the man, however, that he could use the light to help the others make their own torch, and thus by sharing the flame the whole cavern became lit.

One of the disciples asked Hu Song:

'What do we learn by this story?'

Hu Song replied:

'It teaches us that our light remains dark if it is not shared with others. It also tells us that by sharing our light it will not diminish, but on the contrary it will grow.'

Afterward

You Can't Count the Flavor in the Soup (A Collection of Thoughts)

- To work harmoniously with people, with courtesy, respect, and correct manners, is a prerequisite for any achievement in human development. It is as simple and as hard as that.
- The ability to be functional rests on the type of knowledge we work with. Working with information that is useless will not prepare us for encountering our future needs. We must ensure that each of us has the correct tools, the terms of reference, to be efficient for the participation that is required of us.
- Do we fit our intentions into our lives, or do we fit our lives around our intentions?
- The human family is a single organism that connects through the heart. We do not need any secret code or password – we are eligible for our inherent emotional and conscious empowerment by being human.
- The changes we need to see in the world will come: it is the responsibility of those who can – who feel/sense the urge – to do their work by first working on themselves. First, people need to familiarize themselves with certain information.
- Nothing in the world is free: as the aphorism states *Take what you want says God – but pay for it!* In this life everything must be learned. It is our responsibility to make ourselves open and available to learn, whether de-learning, re-learning, or learning anew.
- Old ways, however valuable, are not always automatically the most suitable for what humanity is facing now.
- Many revolutions have been fought in blood for social

change; too few have been fought compassionately for inner development.

- In what we do: is it in service or is it for ourselves?
- Our greatest obstacles to development are anger and fear. Without first achieving balance within ourselves we will not be equipped to move forward in a harmonious and functional manner. We must always begin with ourselves.
- To believe that we live outside of the world of humanity is nothing other than vanity. We are each of us a part of the world, and we are thus compelled to follow and work with the realm of humanity. This is the hardest path, yet one that should not be forgotten. Change must come through human involvement as well as through other means. Each individual is an agent of change, or has the potential to be.
- Don't make things into issues – make them into targets.
- It is important that we embrace ideas now so that they may become acceptable mental currency in advance of their actualization.
- Working with what one instinctively feels to be necessary can be different from working with what one thinks to be important. This distinction is subtle yet often crucial.
- What are we doing here? No one has given me an answer. The truth of it must come from within – I wonder how many of us ask ourselves this question regularly?
- An evolving consciousness reflects the understanding that conscious energy is primary, and the need to be aware and open to ideas and impacts of evolutionary and spiritual thinking. The view that consciousness is a primary force/energy in our reality is the key to helping people expand their consciousness and identify with ever more non-local ties and responsibilities.
- A shaman once said: "A warrior lives by acting, not by thinking about acting, nor by thinking about what he will think when he has finished acting." Today, agents of

change are the new warriors, as hearts in action rather than minds in abstract. Yet this action does not call for a physical demonstration against the incumbent system. Instead, it calls forth an energetic push – a heartfelt impulse – towards an alternative way of being. It is not our aim to be confrontational; rather, it is our aim to be creative.

- We are entering into a world era of greater responsibility. This is not only in terms of our individual actions but reflects also for each thought, emotion, intention, and energetic expression. Increasingly what we manifest within ourselves becomes a part of the external world. This is why we are encouraged to 'become the change we wish to see'. We can each participate in manifesting the change we wish to see in the world around us. This is not metaphysical or occult – it is simply how our integral relationship with the world operates. This relationship is becoming more apparent to a growing number of people as more and more individuals awake to the power of change inherent within each person's mandate of responsibility.

- Each of us helps to support, renew, and rekindle the world through our own separate internal dialogues. It would be helpful if we could consolidate our internal narrative into a unifying, cohesive intent. Now that would be something!

- We should take each step with the knowing that it will count – without doubt or egoism – yet with intent, full personal power, and self-conviction.

- When we 'work' on ourselves we need to do it with a sense of responsibility – just as if we were getting paid for it.

- It is important where one focuses their attention. It takes almost the same energy to make ourselves miserable than it does to make ourselves strong. It is only a matter of personal emphasis. It is our duty to balance the critical nature of our world situation with the joy, wonder, and honor of being alive at this time.

- Respect for others begins first with respect to one's self. If we are unable to achieve this we may find ourselves working to fulfill a self-need rather than working towards selfless action.
- Many people look for a 'Path', a teaching, as an alternative to their current social lives. Not because they necessarily are looking for truth, but because they are unsatisfied socially.
- Individuals do not win victories by banging their heads against walls, but by bypassing them. We can demolish the walls that stand before us by a conscious side-stepping rather than engaging with the old paradigms of conflict and attack.
- No one is born complete or self-attained. Yet we are each born into this world with the possibility to achieve this. How we choose to become, to grow, rests largely upon what we make of ourselves under the given circumstances. It is not so much what happens to us but rather how we respond to our circumstances that determines what we become.
- Challenges are simply challenges, and life is a constant challenge. It helps us to grow within the influences if we do not give ourselves over to complaints and regrets. By lingering too long upon our own judgments we impede our way forward. Self-pity lowers our energy potential and our ability to be an active force in the world. Self-indulgence distracts a person from what they can truly achieve when they are free to focus and concentrate on their intention.
- We are more timid, less courageous, when we are saddled with fears over what we may lose. This is the old paradigm of thought, keeping us tied to struggling against change. We don't like change; it is something new, uncertain, and

involves letting go of something. In this thinking we can never be free enough to move forward openly. The world is constantly moving up and down: each of us, however, must learn how to harmoniously *move through*.

- Don't try to control things; it will only bring more anxiety into life. Trust in those internal movements that will manifest circumstances in life. Such trust embraces an elegant design of what is already to be.

- Some of the old ways of behaving are expecting to be told what to do, and then fighting against not doing what we are told. This is a typical entanglement that entraps and distracts a person from moving forward in the right direction. This is why it is the hardest path to work effectively within the world of people, and also why it is so very necessary.

- It needs to be recognized that a consciousness shift is now underway as the world has come to a point where it cannot continue without a shift in perceptual reality. The world humanity inhabits is, as never before in our recorded history, globally and integrally connected. During this crucial 'phase change' we are experiencing 'perceptual disturbances', as well as Earth changes.

- Human dreams can exercise great power, or they can be passive distractions. Dreams must take on a residue of power, of focused intention, if they are to manifest and exert influence in the physical world.

- This phase of human history is set to end; the parameters are being shifted. And the younger generations instinctively know this – they 'get it' – and are already working to see the shift manifest on this planet within our lifetimes. There is already a world-shift happening.

- Our brains have the biological capacity to form a myriad of local and non-local connections, to adapt and readapt our neurons (re-wiring by re-firing), and to empathize with others through the unconscious firing of our mirror neurons. We also now have technologies that enable us to materially achieve our greater connections – yet we need a worldview, a consciousness and perceptual paradigm to embrace this. We are getting there, but we have not arrived yet.

- We are re-patterning our social relations and forming new modes of interpersonal connections and communications. This will herald a new set of shared values, understanding, empathy, and respect. As a global family we have already suffered enough from existence within an egocentric world, driven by cravings of power, greed, and control. These institutions are now archaic and destructive to our continued survival. They are the dregs of an old mode of existence, one that is unsuitable for a world to come.

- The ideal set of relations would be that which honored the Golden Rule; exchanges on mutual trust and respect. We may be a long way from this, yet the seeds have been planted, and are growing in firm soil around the world – in projects, communities, networks... the new Renaissance will not emerge from the center like the previous one that sprung up in Florence in the Late Middle Ages... it will come from the periphery, a distributed and network emergence of conscious individuals and groupings. Like ink dots on blotting paper, these conscious and creative centers will spread their influence throughout the networks until a time will come when the ink dots begin to fill the blotting paper.

- The new Renaissance will be a decentralized movement – a movement from the people; a shift catalyzed within the hearts, spirit, and minds of the people. Mass connectivity will require a greater sense of resonance between all humans. Resonance, a vibratory force, gradually retunes those in its field into a shared harmonic. Human beings are both individually and collectively resonating tools. In our changing times we will increasingly be reaching out to those who attract us, with whom we can communicate, and to likeminded people. We will instinctively feel the rising need to connect with others who feel, sense, and think as us.

- As a species we are beginning to fuse; we are still fragmented and rife with cracks and schisms. These have often been deliberate policies of control – divide and conquer – which are now being overridden by a new program: a program of respect and unite. Our schisms will eventually bring us closer together, as we collectively transform the brutalities of the old world systems.

- We are called to respond differently to the world around us – not in fear or with anxiety, with trepidation or appre-hension; but with robustness, energy, flexibility creativity, and positive intentions. The world in which we live is an ecology of which we are a part – we must learn to respect this, to feel it, and to develop our lives around it. It is our duty to be responsive in a functional yet compassionate manner, with understanding and knowledge; with action and inaction; with exertion and with patience. We must learn when *to do* and when *to be*.

- We should be mindful and aware of our own transfor-mation; how each day brings new impacts, emotions, learning opportunities. We live in a vast, dynamic, living school – nothing is static. We are not machines, robotic automations that respond to applied stimuli. We are complex emotional and spiritual beings that have a myriad of encounters, events, and experiences from which to learn, grow, and evolve. We should strive to always remember this, to avoid those things that pacify us, that dull our senses and make us feel small and worthless. We are energetic beings. We are here now to be empowered, not suppressed, oppressed, nor repressed.

- Current social breakdowns and crises are catalyzing innovations, creative systems, and humanitarian networking. When the center begins to implode under its own weighty inefficiency, the periphery gains regenerative energies.

- Change will come through the living spirit of people. When a sincere intention is placed into the world, it can, and does, move matter into its alignment.

- Just as the communications revolution catalyzed a global consciousness, so too will a consciousness revolution impact our collective spiritual hearts – this will be the true mark of the maturity of our species. No true sense of physical unity (nation blocs – planetary society) can come into being if we are unable to cultivate and nurture the 'being' of unity within our very own internal states.

- Inner resolve and balance can be a powerful ally to sheer willpower. Our internal state is a measure of our own strength, forbearance, and fortitude. We need to cultivate this focus, this ability for calmness within change and adversity, in order to manage our maturity into the next phase of our evolutionary development.

- The meaning of humanity can be said to be evolutionary. Each person has the capacity to 'polish the connection' between themselves and a living, energetic universe.

- The ultimate revolution needed on this planet of ours is a spiritual revolution; that is, a revolution in our inner gnosis, understanding, and our inherent conscious selves – an opening up and further development of our spiritual dimension.

- If we live our lives purely externally without an inner dimension we will be lacking in the full and complete development of qualities needed to bring a harmonious and sustainable long-term future into being.

- It is important that a person acquires the ability to correctly assess or measure: i) what they need; ii) how to go about achieving it; iii) what is true; and iv) what is false. Many people falsely believe they know all of these things, when in fact it is usually the case that these things are only understood in a limited sense.

- The human need to struggle and be successful – to progress in life – is the manifestation of an evolutionary imperative. However, it is only a secondary expression of this essential urge. To fully develop as a human being, we are called upon to focus on its primary manifestation: the evolutionary imperative within each of us to develop our conscious self.

- Sincerity – with others and with oneself – is one of the few tools we have for gaining our personal freedom.

- We continually hear calls for us to 'wake up'; that humanity is 'asleep', etc – yet seldom are we told that once awake we need to have the means to profit from this wakefulness. Such preparation is as much important as the waking itself.

- Most people want to learn, yet only in a manner laid down by them – or in a way that is emotionally satisfying to them.

- Each person should decide for themselves if they are actively looking for intellectual and emotional stimulus. If so, then such things can be found – indeed, are offered – all around us. Yet they may have little or no developmental value.

- We all too easily adopt relative truths and sanctify them as idols. This lack of perception effectively blocks access for the appearance and application of absolute, objective truths.

- What may help us at one stage of our lives may hinder us at another. We should be open to evaluation at all times and to learn to recognize this difference.

- It is a human tendency to take constructive ideas and turn them into recreational toys. Thus, when playing they are able to tell themselves they are involved in 'higher things'. That is why cults are so numerous in human cultures. Also, why mimicry is lauded as a worthy endeavour.

- We should strengthen our capacity to see beyond paradoxes; to perceive the harmony within inconsistent things.

- Beliefs are not facts: a belief is a belief because it is neither knowledge nor truth. It is a conviction of faith—a thought backed by emotional attachment.

- We need to know and to feel that we have the spiritual impulse running through us and that it runs through every aspect of our physical lives.

- When conscience and genuine intuition are operating together there is an intention that is not thought, wish, or an object. It is an intention that can override the thoughts of conditioning.

- Mental stabilization and social harmony are not ways to higher consciousness but rather the very necessary needs of our basic functioning. These are our minimal requirements, not our end goals.

- Knowledge shares itself with those who approach it in the correct way.

- The world we are moving into requires of us that we both inspire and be inspired.

APPENDIX

1. Spirituality vs. Fetishism

Much of what contemporary societies take to be 'spirituality' - rituals, talismans, practices, etc – have either been imported from elsewhere, appropriated from earlier forms, or become atrophied, frozen into symbol and peddled as emotional stimuli. Does this sound harsh?

Well, what is often the case is that many once-legitimate spiritual practices have lost their functionality as they have been removed from their original context. When such precise tools are used in a haphazard way they are in danger of becoming incantations at best, or conditioners at worst. When such symbols of 'higher learning' become atrophied – meaning they are no longer adapted to the culture, the time, and the people – they often incite a 'Pavlovian' dog response from the part of the practitioners. It is a situation of emotional stimuli creating a wishful and often gratifying automatic reply. Such tools that perhaps once had a very precise function within a specific time and context are easily transferred into fetish totems.

People with a genuine wish to find a path of inner development can find themselves vulnerable to such unconscious, or deliberate, mechanisms. When under deliberate manipulation these emotional icons can lead people into feelings of contentment, maybe even ego-based satisfaction, yet they are not the basis for any real learning.

Spirituality involves the correct employment of precise procedures at specific stages. It is not about excitement; rather, it involves having the right knowledge and information to know what is needed. It is not a road of wishes, but a path of needs and capacity.

Often what we see as cultural forms of 'spirituality' are little other than conditioning techniques. It may be a case that the original impulse has outlived its context and usefulness; or it applies to another culture in which it was projected; or that the representatives of it have chosen to 'mix-n-match' various techniques to form something which is appealing and 'holistic'. In all these ways, the real inner function of the teaching has been lost.

Spirituality has become its own marketplace in the modern world; much like the Pardoners of old would sell forgiveness of sins for a price. The responsibility rests with the individual to have a focused and attentive interior filtering mechanism. Are we searching for emotional stimuli and satisfaction? Are we unconsciously wanting to find a community to replace a lack in our social lives? Or do we truly need a precise, functioning process of inner development?

The blind imitation of practices that are often sold to us as spiritual techniques may seem harmless. Yet the misdirection of our needs, and the denial of proper nourishment, can leave a person not only vulnerable to exploitation but also starving of correct nourishment.

We are living in times where there is both a great deal of empowering energy and awareness exploding, stimulating people to re-evaluate their purpose, direction, and sense of self. At the same time, for many of us, we are living in social environments that are eclectic, consumerist, commercial, and offering exorbitant choice in the belief that more is good. This encourages some people to take, experiment, taste, and dabble with a rag-bag bunch of spiritual goodies in the hope that the resulting fusion will 'do some good'. This, it seems, is a rather complex way for something which begins simply – with the self.

Life offers the entire stimulus we need; there is no need for us to seek out more. Likewise, it is not necessary that we retreat to a cave in order to escape this sensory overload. Any true spiritual endeavour has to be in harmony with one's life. If there is friction, and incompatibility with a normal, balanced life, then we must ask serious questions about the 'spirituality' we are following. There should not be an 'either/or' issue surrounding one's inner development. To work on oneself entails that we also work in life. This is the only way to form a balanced, harmonious, integrated self.

There is a story which tells of a spiritual seeker who after some time comes upon a spiritual master that she feels is genuine and whom she wishes to learn from. The seeker asks the master if he will accept her as a pupil.

'Why do you seek a spiritual path?' asks the teacher.

'Because I wish to be a generous and virtuous person; I wish to be balanced, mindful, caring, and to be in service for humanity. This is my goal' said the seeker.

'Well', replied the teacher, 'these are not goals on the spiritual path; these are the very basics of being human which we need before we even begin to learn'.

Modern society is an 'on-demand' life where we are used to receiving that which we request – a demand-supply conditioning. Because of this we are often at the mercy of the conveyor belt of spiritual-supply. Yet the first steps should begin with a person having a dialogue with themselves. We *sense* a lot of the answers; we have very refined filters within us that can, if we activate them, filter out much of the rubbish that comes our way.

Then we need information. What is an active, correct projection of inner transformation in *my culture at this current time*? We don't need to learn Sanskrit to make contact with an active path of development. We only need to lose our conditioning for emotional stimulation, attachment to archaic yet appealing rituals, and our fetishism for talismans and exotic objects. Obsessive tendencies for the garb of 'something higher' are little other than fixation of greed and a form of lower-level indoctrination.

We would do well to consider that the 'spiritual', as we have come to call it, is none other than necessary human nutrition, a daily requirement for living. Yet like eating and breathing, it has to be correctly integrated into our lives without making a song and dance about it. And, of course, not forgetting that:

'If you insist on buying poor food, you must be prepared to dislike it at the serving'

2. Spirituality vs. Consumerism

Ritual is important, yet often it is least beneficial to those people who are ritualistically-minded and inclined to habit. The word 'tradition' is now applied to many socially embedded religious and 'spiritual' practices that have become engrained within our cultures. Yet in many instances it is possible to replace the notion of 'tradition' with 'repetition'. Certain beliefs and practices are passed on through the generations without modification or adaption to circumstances such as the current time and place of operation. This is little more than repetition of a fixed formula that whilst was functioning in its time, is often now without its inner kinetic energy. It can be said to be like the shell of an oyster that has long been bereft of its pearl.

An example of this can be seen in this interchange between a genuine spiritual teacher who went to an Asiatic country to address the issue of repetition. The visitor explained to the incumbent sheik that the practices he was advocating belonged to a time in the past and were limited for a specific, targeted audience. Since such conditions no longer existed, what remained was merely an outer core – a spectacle. The old Sheikh, who was the head of the order, replied that 'in a world where there is no light at all, even a false gleam is perhaps something to have', and that 'I have been here so long, and so have my ancestors, that we cannot change.' The old sheikh continued with his refusal by further adding that 'we may well be wanted, and believed to be the possessors of secrets…we are here, after seven hundred years, not because of our value or viciousness, but because people want us. They want magic…many can follow a harmless path and feel better, elevated. That, in any case, is what they imagine spirituality to be.'iv

However, imagining what 'spirituality to be' is like, is similar to imagining that the air we breathe is one substance. Yet this is not so, for if we have knowledge of the correct composition of a substance we find that it is composed of many elements in specific alignment and concentration. To focus on only a part of the substance and to gain nutrition from this, such as from ritual or selected practices only, is not only inefficient yet potentially harmful. Using this analogy for the air we breath, we know from science that air is composed of 21% oxygen, 78% nitrogen, and 1% of other gases including argon and carbon dioxide. Yet if a person decided to select the nitrogen component only, and to concentrate their 'ritual' breathing on this part alone they would not find themselves breathing at all after very long.

Spiritual practices in the modern world are rife with repetition; mainly because repetition reinforces mental, emotional, and physical conditioning and patterns of behaviour. Further, repetition in such 'spiritual practices' often involve the carrying on of selected elements; that is, those elements which it has been decided upon will be most useful to pass on and highlight. In such cases we need to ask – on whose authority? If one has a headache we may take an aspirin, yet to repeat this a hundred times will have a different effect than making the headache go away…we may lose much more!

Repetition in the science of inner transformation can be damaging if it is not in correct proportion to the whole. Each of us has a capacity to recognize that which is genuine; only that often it is clouded beneath an array of acquired traits such as laziness, greed, etc. One way to cut through this is to be sincere with oneself - to ask oneself directly if what you are doing is truly providing the nourishment and development required. If there is a need for self-justification then we might ask ourselves why?

Just as in recent years the credit bubble placed many people into a false sense of security by offering the possibility to obtain untold goodies, so too does the promise of repetitious and ritualistic forms of spirituality. Many were duped into 'repetitious consumerism' because of the offering of cheap credit ('false gold'). Likewise, many people are also attracted to the window-displays of attractive practices of inner transformation. Quotations and phrases are consumed and put on display; deeds are admired and miracles invoked. Even the extremes are commercialized: ritual suffering; automatic obedience; reward and punishment, etc. Yet all are low-level emotional stimulus. As one contemporary teacher commented: 'The would-be learner, instead of realizing that there is an objective, becomes a bemused consumer of wonders and stimuli'. Such offerings may be 'consumable', yet are they part of a disciplined science that forms a unified, complete teaching of aligned development in recognition of specific contexts? As the saying goes – 'False gold exists only because real gold exists'.

The inner evolutionary imperative is not a shopping list, or the random acquisition of abilities, nor the gaining of emotional satisfaction. It is a genuine inner need that, if acted upon sincerely and with genuine intention, can be of immense benefit to the individual and to the planet.

'Falsely spiritual people are easily seen through, because they think, like materialists, in transactionalist terms. They want to get something in exchange for something else.' (Idries Shah)

Annotated References

1   Frankl, V.E. (1997) *Man's Search for Meaning*. New York: Pocket Books

2   Shah, I. (1982) *The Sufis*. London: Octagon

3   Birkbeck, L. (2008) *Understanding the Future*. London: Watkins

4   See Laszlo, E. (2006) *The Chaos Point: The World at the Crossroads*. Charlottesville, VA: Hampton Roads

5   Taken from *Four Quartets* by T.S. Eliot

6   Shah, I. (1969) *Reflections*. London: Octagon Press

7   Castaneda, C. (1999) *The Wheel of Time*. London: Allen Lane

8   Frankl, VE (1997) *Man's Search for Meaning*. New York: Pocket Books

9   Shah, I. (1969) *Reflections*. London: Octagon Press

10   Cited in Baines, J. (2002 – 2nd Edition) *The Stellar Man (Hermetic Philosophy, Bk 2)*. New York: John Baines Institute

11   Toch, H. (1965) *The Social Psychology Of Social Movements*. Indianapolis: Bobbs-Merrill Co

12   Winn, D. (1983) *The Manipulated Mind*. London: Octagon Press

13   Toch, H. (1965) *The Social Psychology Of Social Movements*. Indianapolis: Bobbs-Merrill Co

14   Winn, D. (1983) *The Manipulated Mind*. London: Octagon Press

15   Shah, I. (1969) *Reflections*. London: Octagon Press

16   Baines, J. (2002 – 2nd. Edition) *The Stellar Man (Hermetic Philosophy, Bk 2)*. New York: John Baines Institute

17   Becker, R.O. (1998) *The Body Electric*. New York: William Morrow

18   Black, J. (2008) *The Secret History of the World*. London: Quercus Publishing

19   See Fromm, E. (1960) *The Fear of Freedom*. London: Routledge

& Kegan Paul

20 Shah, I. (1980) *The Way of the Sufi*. London: Octagon Press

21 See Csikszentmihalyi, M. (1993) *The Evolving Self: A Psychology for the Third Millennium*. New York: HarperCollins

22 The author's own poem dated 17/8/95

23 Birkbeck, L. (2008) *Understanding the Future*. London: Watkins

24 Three Initiates (2008) *The Kybalion*. London: Tarcher

25 Three Initiates (2008) *The Kybalion*. London: Tarcher

26 Castaneda, C. (1999) *The Wheel of Time*. London: Allen Lane

27 Three Initiates (2008) *The Kybalion*. London: Tarcher

28 Shah, I. (1971) *Thinkers of the East*. London: Jonathan Cape

29 Shah, I. (1971) *Thinkers of the East*. London: Jonathan Cape

30 Shah, I. (1982) *Tales of the Dervishes*. London: Octagon Press

31 Three Initiates (2008) *The Kybalion*. London: Tarcher

32 Sanai, H. (1974) *The Walled Garden of Truth*. London: Octagon Press

33 Winn, D. (1983) *The Manipulated Mind*. London: Octagon Press

34 Ali-Shah, O. (1998) *The Rules or Secrets of the Naqshbandi Order*. Paris: Tractus Books

35 Three Initiates (2008) *The Kybalion*. London: Tarcher

36 Three Initiates (2008) *The Kybalion*. London: Tarcher

37 Sanai, H. (1974) *The Walled Garden of Truth*. London: Octagon Press

i Shah, I. (1982) *Seeker After Truth*. London: Octagon

ii See Stanley Milgram's famous experiments on 'Obedience to Authority'

iii A 13th century Persian poet

iv John Grant, '*Travels in the Unknown East*', Octagon Press, 1992

BOOKS

O is a symbol of the world, of oneness and unity. In different cultures it also means the "eye," symbolizing knowledge and insight. We aim to publish books that are accessible, constructive and that challenge accepted opinion, both that of academia and the "moral majority."

Our books are available in all good English language bookstores worldwide. If you don't see the book on the shelves ask the bookstore to order it for you, quoting the ISBN number and title. Alternatively you can order online (all major online retail sites carry our titles) or contact the distributor in the relevant country, listed on the copyright page.

See our website www.o-books.net for a full list of over 500 titles, growing by 100 a year.

And tune in to myspiritradio.com for our book review radio show, hosted by June-Elleni Laine, where you can listen to the authors discussing their books.

MySpiritRadio